John Muir

In His Own Words

A Book of Quotations

Compiled and edited by

Peter Browning

Great West Books   Lafayette, California

Cover design by Larry B. Van Dyke
Cover photographs: Courtesy, The Bancroft Library

Manufactured in the United States of America

Eighth printing, July 2009

Great West Books
PO Box 1028
Lafayette, CA 94549
Phone & Fax: (925) 283-3184
E-mail: peter@greatwestbooks.com
Website: http://www.greatwestbooks.com

Library of Congress Cataloging-in-Publication Data

Muir, John, 1838–1914.
    John Muir in his own words.

    Includes index.
        1. Muir, John, 1838–1914. 2. Natural history—
United States. 3. Nature conservation—United States.
4. Naturalists—United States—Biography.
I. Browning, Peter, 1928–   . II. Title.
QH31.M9A3 1988   508.794   87–83325
ISBN 0–944220–02–9 (pbk. : alk. paper)

Contents

Introduction

If one were to use John Muir's published writings to illuminate his thought and literary development in the usual lineal manner—from youth to old age—the first volume would be *The Story of My Boyhood and Youth*. But that would be quite misleading, since Muir wrote that book late in life. It has the distinctive tone and content that mark the retrospective, autobiographical view. Muir was saying *now* what he thought and felt *then*. He used the vocabulary and style he had developed over several decades of writing for publication. His perceptions of early life inevitably were colored and slanted by the experiences of a lifetime. It was not a false view of his life, but it most certainly was not what he would have written—assuming the ability—at age fifteen or twenty.

To the best of *my* ability I have arranged the quotations in this book chronologically. The chronology is meant to reflect the order in which they were written rather than what period of life they are about or when they were first published. Thus the quotations from *The Story of My Boyhood and Youth* are well toward the end of the book. Large portions of that volume were published serially in the *Atlantic Monthly* from November 1912 through February 1913, and the book itself was published in March 1913.

Muir's earliest writings—aside from personal letters—were his journals. The first journal, which covered his walk to the Gulf of Mexico in 1867 and up until his arrival in San Francisco in March 1868, was published in 1916—almost two years after his death—as *A Thousand-Mile Walk to the Gulf*.

The volume *My First Summer in the Sierra*, published in 1911, was Muir's first use of his journals: the record of his experiences, thoughts, and emotions while he worked as a sheepherder during the spring and summer of 1869.

Anyone who starts at the beginning of this book and reads it straight through will see the changes in style and content. In his early journals Muir was concerned with the momentous questions that come to everyone: Who am I? Where am I going? What's it all about? What will become of me? Those questions were answered by his first summer in the Sierra. Soon thereafter he established himself in Yosemite Valley, and when he began to write for publication in the early 1870s he was more focused on the outer world than on himself. He wrote in glowing terms about the magnificence of the mountains and the beauty of the flora and fauna. He insisted that all people would be made well and whole if only they would come to his glorious mountains— and when the crowds of tourists arrived he was scornful of their apathy and their reluctance to shed their urban habits. A strong element of social criticism appeared in his articles, and as he became the foremost conservationist of his time it was inevitable that his writing would reflect the political battles he was involved in. As a true believer, Muir preached and proselytized and banged the drums for his dearest beliefs.

A great deal of what Muir wrote appeared in more than one publication. A number of his books are collections of articles and essays that originally were published in newspapers and magazines. He often rewrote passages that were to be republished—sometimes improving them and sometimes not. I have tried to locate the first instance of every quotation in this book, and I have used the exact wording and punctuation of that first version. As the reader will discover, upon encountering a quotation in a later publication, the wording and punctuation may well have been altered. In the citation that follows each quotation I have put the date it was written, if that could be determined. In some instances the only date is that of publication, since the date it actually was written could not be established. Following the date is information on when and where the passage was first published. If it later was reprinted in one of the books, that work is cited last. In a reference to any of the books, whether it be a primary or a secondary reference, the page number given is from the first edition; reprint editions may well have different pagination. For the sake of keeping the citations to a reasonable length, I have used three-letter abbreviations for all the books. They are, with the year of publication:

BAY	*The Story of My Boyhood and Youth, 1913*
COC	*The Cruise of the Corwin, 1917*
JOM	*John of the Mountains, 1938*
LAL	*The Life and Letters of John Muir, 1924*
LTF	*Letters to a Friend, 1915*
MFS	*My First Summer in the Sierra, 1911*
MOC	*The Mountains of California, 1894*
ONP	*Our National Parks, 1901*
SIS	*Studies in the Sierra, 1950*
SKN	*Stickeen, 1909*
STT	*Steep Trails, 1918*
TIA	*Travels in Alaska, 1915*
TMW	*A Thousand-Mile Walk to the Gulf, 1916*
YOS	*The Yosemite, 1912*

Muir died on Christmas Eve of 1914. Only six of these books were published during his lifetime. Five were published during the four years after his death. The contents of *Letters to a Friend* had been selected by Muir. He was working on *Travels in Alaska* at the time of his death; the manuscript was completed by Marion Randall Parsons.

Dr. William Frederic Badè, Muir's literary executor, edited *A Thousand-Mile Walk to the Gulf* and *The Cruise of the Corwin*. The book *Steep Trails* is a collection of Muir's articles from newspapers and magazines, and also includes three essays he wrote for the book *Picturesque California and the Region West of the Rocky Mountains,* of which he was the editor.

Badè collected and edited the letters for *The Life and Letters of John Muir*. Linnie Marsh Wolfe edited *John of the Mountains, the Unpublished Journals of John Muir*. The volume *Studies in the Sierra* was first published as a book by the Sierra Club in 1950. The essays in that book originally appeared as a series in *Overland Monthly* in 1874, and were reprinted in the *Sierra Club Bulletin* between 1915 and 1921.

Since I have endeavored to present these quotations in chronological order, quotations from a given book may be widely separated. For those who may wish to locate all the quotations from one book, no matter when or where they first appeared, the following list of quotation numbers should make that possible.

The Cruise of the Corwin - 190–94, 196
John of the Mountains - 28–29, 31–33, 77–79, 85, 87–96, 101, 107, 110–20, 122, 126–27, 131–35, 142, 153–59, 188, 221–28, 234–36, 276, 280, 325–29
Letters to a Friend - 2–3, 5, 25–27, 30, 34, 74–75, 80–82, 106, 125
The Life and Letters of John Muir - 1, 76, 83–84, 86, 102–4, 108–9, 121, 136, 141, 166, 175, 187, 197, 218, 275, 282, 284, 309–12,
The Mountains of California - 160, 162, 167, 170–72, 186, 195, 229–32
My First Summer in the Sierra - 35–73
Our National Parks - 244–54, 260–74, 277–79, 281, 283, 285–86
Studies in the Sierra - 128–130, 143–44
Steep Trails - 145–52, 163–65, 173, 199–215, 287–91, 332
Stickeen - 255–57
The Story of My Boyhood and Youth - 302–8, 313–24
A Thousand-Mile Walk to the Gulf - 4, 6–24
Travels in Alaska - 180–84, 219–220
The Yosemite - 189, 198, 292, 294–96, 299–301

At first I arranged the quotations in quite a different order. I took the path of least resistance, and simply clustered them according to the volume in which they appeared. At the end of the manuscript I had a sizable miscellaneous section, where I put all the quotations from various sources that had not been collected in one of the books. When I became dissatisfied with this arrangement, and decided to organize the quotations chronologically, I faced what might well have been the insuperable problem of trying to trace more than two hundred passages back to their sources. In the event, it was a time-consuming task, but it was made possible by the existence of a superb reference work. My constant companion in this chore was the second edition of *John Muir, A Reading Bibliography*, by William F. Kimes and Maymie B. Kimes. (Fresno: Panorama est Books, 1986.) The authors have created a detailed and wonderfully cross-referenced work that leads the user forward or backward from any point, naming the antecedents and descendants of every condensed, expanded, and rearranged article, essay, and letter that has been published. Muir's custom of reworking and rearranging his material can easily leave an innocent researcher utterly confused as to the provenance of any given passage. Without the invaluable assistance of William and Maymie Kimes I might still be out in the bush, thrashing around in a Muir-created wilderness.

Every book, on whatever subject, had its beginning in someone's head—a "brainstorm" as the vernacular has it. This particular tempest occurred in the mind of Barbara Lekisch some six or seven years ago, when she was the librarian at the Sierra Club. It was also she who introduced me to *John Muir, A Reading Bibliography*, so I am doubly indebted.

What if the Indians are exterminated, are not savages as grim prowling about the clearings today?

The universe is wider than our views of it.

—Thoreau

So Little a Time

1860–1869

1

A body has an extraordinary amount of longfaced sober scheming and thought to get butter and bread. (Letter to his sister Sarah, fall of 1860; *LAL*, vol. 1, 82.)

2

. . . A lifetime is so little a time that we die before we get ready to live. I should like to study at a college, but then I have to say to myself: "You will die before you can do anything else." (Letter to Mrs. Carr, September 13, 1866; *The Craftsman*, March 1905, 643; *LTF*, 9.)

3

I was struck with your remarks about our real little home of stillness and peace. How little does the outer and noisy world know of that "real home" and real inner life! Happy indeed they who have a friend to whom they can unmask the workings of their real life, sure of sympathy and forbearance! (Letter to Mrs. Carr, September 13, 1866; *LTF,* 11.)

4

Few bodies are inhabited by so satisfied a soul as to be allowed exemption from extraordinary exertion through a whole life. (From Muir's journal, 1867; *TMW*, Introduction, xiv; *LAL*, vol. 1, 158.)

5

I wish I knew where I was going. Doomed to be "carried of the spirit into the wilderness," I suppose. I wish I could be more

moderate in my desires, but I cannot, and so there is no rest.
(Letter to Mrs. Carr, August 30, 1867; *LTF*, 32.)

6

He was one of those useful, practical men—too wise to waste
precious time with weeds, caves, fossils, or anything else that he
could not eat. (1867; Kentucky Forests and Caves, *TMW*, 10–11.)

7

I never before saw Nature's grandeur in so abrupt contrast
with paltry artificial gardens. The fashionable hotel grounds are
in exact parlor taste, with many a beautiful plant cultivated to
deformity, and arranged in strict geometrical beds, the whole
pretty affair a laborious failure side by side with Divine beauty.
(1867; Kentucky Forests and Caves, *TMW*, 11–12.)

8

[I] escaped from a heap of uncordial kindness to the generous
bosom of the woods. (1867; Kentucky Forests and Caves, *TMW*,
15–16.)

9

You . . . are with Nature in the grand old forest graveyard, so
beautiful that almost any sensible person would choose to dwell
here with the dead rather than with the lazy, disorderly living.
(1867; Camping Among the Tombs, *TMW*, 67.)

10

Bonaventure is called a graveyard, a town of the dead, but the
few graves are powerless in such a depth of life. The rippling of
living waters, the song of birds, the joyous confidence of flowers,
the calm, undisturbable grandeur of the oaks, mark this place of
graves as one of the Lord's most favored abodes of life and light.
(1867; Camping Among the Tombs, *TMW*, 69.)

11

On no subject are our ideas more warped and pitiable than
on death. Instead of the sympathy, the friendly union, of life
and death so apparent in Nature, we are taught that death is an
accident, a deplorable punishment for the oldest sin, the arch-
enemy of life. (1867; Camping Among the Tombs, *TMW*, 70.)

12

. . . How assiduously Nature seeks to remedy these labored art blunders. She corrodes the iron and marble, and gradually levels the hill which is always heaped up, as if a sufficiently heavy quantity of clods could not be laid upon the dead. Arching grasses come one by one; seeds come flying on downy wings, silent as fate, to give life's dearest beauty for the ashes of art; and strong evergreen arms laden with ferns and tillandsia drapery are spread over all—Life at work everywhere, obliterating all memory of the confusion of man. (1867; Camping Among the Tombs, *TMW*, 71–72.)

13

A serious matter is this bread which perishes, and, could it be dispensed with, I doubt if civilization would ever see me again. (1867; Florida Swamps and Forests, *TMW*, 95; Muir's thought after going without breakfast.)

14

How narrow we selfish, conceited creatures are in our sympathies! how blind to the rights of all the rest of creation! (1867; Florida Swamps and Forests, *TMW*, 98.)

15

Most streams appear to travel through a country with thoughts and plans for something beyond. But those of Florida are at home, do not appear to be traveling at all, and seem to know nothing of the sea. (1867; Florida Swamps and Forests, *TMW*, 101.)

16

How strangely we are blinded to beauty and color, form and motion, by comparative size! For example, we measure grasses by our own stature and by the height and bulkiness of trees. But what is the size of the greatest man, or the tallest tree that ever overtopped a grass! Compared with other things in God's creation the difference is nothing. (1867; Florida Swamps and Forests, *TMW*, 102–3.)

17

These little fenced fields look as if they were intended to be for plants what cages are for birds. (1867; Florida Swamps and Forests, *TMW*, 105.)

18

There is that in the glance of a flower which may at times control the greatest of creation's braggart lords. (1867; Florida Swamps and Forests, *TMW*, 108.)

19

I have seen dirt on garments regularly stratified, the various strata no doubt indicating different periods of life. Some of them perhaps, were annual layers, furnishing, like those of trees, a means of determining the age. Man and other civilized animals are the only creatures that ever become dirty. (1867; Florida Swamps and Forests, *TMW*, 110.)

20

To me it appeared as "d——dest" work to slaughter God's cattle for sport. "They were made for us," say these self-approving preachers; "for our food, our recreation, or other uses not yet discovered." As truthfully we might say on behalf of a bear, when he deals successfully with an unfortunate hunter, "Men and other bipeds were made for bears, and thanks be to God for claws and teeth so long." (1867; Florida Swamps and Forests, *TMW*, 122.)

21

We cannot forget anything. Memories may escape the action of will, may sleep a long time, but when stirred by the right influence . . . they flash into full stature and life with everything in place. (1867; Cedar Keys, *TMW*, 124.)

22

The world, we are told, was made especially for man—a presumption not supported by all the facts. A numerous class of men are painfully astonished whenever they find anything, living or dead, in all God's universe, which they cannot eat or render in some way what they call useful to themselves. They have precise dogmatic insight of the intentions of the Creator,

and it is hardly possible to be guilty of irreverence in speaking
of *their* God any more than of heathen idols. He is regarded as
a civilized gentleman in favor either of a republican form of
government or of a limited monarchy; believes in the literature
and language of England; is a warm supporter of the English
constitution and Sunday schools and missionary societies; and is
as purely a manufactured article as any puppet of a half-penny
theater. (1867; Cedar Keys, *TMW*, 136–37.)

23

There is not a fragment in all nature, for every relative
fragment of one thing is a full harmonious unit in itself.
(1867; A Sojourn in Cuba, *TMW*, 164.)

24

. . . No one can tell how far our star may finally be subdued
to man's will. (1867 or 1868; To California, *TMW*, 179.)

25

I am well again, I came to life in the cool winds and crystal
waters of the mountains . . . . (Letter to Mrs. Carr, July 26, 1868;
LTF, 37.)

26

. . . The sky was delicious—sweet enough for the breath of
angels. Every draught of it gave a separate and distinct piece of
pleasure. I do not believe that Adam and Eve ever tasted better
in their balmiest nook. (Letter to Mrs. Carr, July 26, 1868; *The
Craftsman*, March 1905, 645; *LTF*, 38.)

27

I am sure you will be directed by Providence to the place
where you will best serve the end of existence. (Letter to Mrs.
Carr, November 1, 1868; *LTF*, 48.)

28

There are no unwritten pages in Nature, but everywhere line
upon line. In like manner every human heart and mind is written
upon as created . . . . Happy is the man who is so engraved that
when he reaches the calm days of reflection he may rejoice in

following the forms of both his upper and under lines.
(At Smoky Jack's Sheep Camp, January 4, 1869; *JOM,* 11.)

29

If the Creator were to bestow a new set of senses upon us, or slightly remodel the present ones, leaving all the rest of nature unchanged, we should never doubt we were in another world, and so in strict reality we should be, just as if all the world besides our senses were changed. (At Smoky Jack's Sheep Camp, January 6, 1869; *JOM,* 12.)

30

Pure science is a most unmarketable commodity in California. Conspicuous, energetic, unmixed materialism rules supreme in all classes. (Letter to Mrs. Carr, February 24, 1869; *LTF,* 50.)

Going to the Mountains

1869

31

Killed a rattlesnake that was tranquilly sunning himself in coiled ease about a bunch of grass. After dislodging him by throwing dirt, I killed him by jumping upon him, because no stones or sticks were near. He defended himself bravely, and I ought to have been bitten. He was innocent and deserved life. (At Smoky Jack's Sheep Camp, March 14, 1869; *JOM,* 28.)

32

After an experience of a hundred days, I cannot find the poetry of a shepherd's life apart from Nature. If ancient shepherds were so intelligent and lute-voiced, why are modern ones in the Lord's grandest gardens usually so muddy and degraded? . . . Milton in his darkness bewailed the absence of 'flocks and herds,' but I am sure that if all the flocks and herds, together with all the other mongrel victims of civilization, were hidden from me, I should rejoice beyond the possibility of any note of wail. (At Smoky Jack's Sheep Camp, March 20, 1869; *JOM,* 29.)

33

The death of flowers in this garden is only change from one form of beauty to another. (At Smoky Jack's Sheep Camp, May 2, 1869; *JOM,* 32.)

34

It would be far more pleasant to camp out . . . than to travel by rule and make forced marches to fixed points of common

resort and common confusion. (Letter to Mrs. Carr, May 16, 1869;
LTF, 56.)

35

We are now in the mountains and they are in us, kindling
enthusiasm, making every nerve quiver, filling every pore and
cell of us. . . . How glorious a conversion, so complete and
wholesome it is, scarce memory enough of old bondage days
left as a standpoint to view it from! In this newness of life we
seem to have been so always. (June 6, 1869; *MFS*, 20–21.)

36

Here I could stay tethered forever with just bread and water,
nor would I be lonely; loved friends and neighbors, as love for
everything increased, would seem all the nearer however many
the miles and mountains between us. (June 6, 1869; *MFS*, 29.)

37

The California sheep-owner is in haste to get rich. . . . Large
flocks may be kept at slight expense, and large profits realized,
the money invested doubling, it is said, every other year. This
quickly acquired wealth usually creates desire for more. Then
indeed the wool is drawn close down over the poor fellows'
eyes, dimming or shutting out almost everything worth seeing.
(June 7, 1869; *Atlantic Monthly*, January 1911, 5; *MFS*, 30.)

38

. . . The California shepherd, so far as I've seen or heard, is
never quite sane for any considerable time. Of all Nature's voices
ba-a is about all he hears. Even the howls and kiyis of coyotes
might be blessings if well heard, but he hears them only through
a blur of mutton and wool, and they do him no good. (June 7,
1869; *Atlantic Monthly*, January 1911, 6; *MFS*, 32–33.)

39

Another glorious Sierra day in which one seems to be
dissolved and absorbed and sent pulsing onward we know not
where. Life seems neither long nor short, and we take no more
heed to save time or make haste than do the trees and stars.
This is true freedom, a good practical sort of immortality.
(June 13, 1869; *Atlantic Monthly*, January 1911, 7; *MFS*, 52.)

40

Only spread a fern-frond over a man's head, and worldly cares are cast out, and freedom and beauty and peace come in. (June 13, 1869; *Atlantic Monthly*, January 1911, 8; *MFS*, 54.)

41

The Digger Indians also are fond of the larvae and even of the perfect ants, so I have been told by old mountaineers. They bite off and reject the head, and eat the tickly acid body with keen relish. Thus are the poor biters bitten, like every other biter, big or little, in the world's great family. (June 13, 1869; *Atlantic Monthly*, January 1911, 10; *MFS*, 61.)

42

How many mouths Nature has to fill, how many neighbors we have, how little we know about them, and seldom we get in each other's way! (June 13, 1869; *Atlantic Monthly*, January 1911, 10; *MFS*, 62.)

43

Indians walk softly and hurt the landscape hardly more than the birds and squirrels, and their brush and bark huts last hardly longer than those of wood rats, while their more enduring monuments . . . vanish in a few centuries.

How different are most of those of the white man . . . roads blasted in the solid rock, wild streams dammed and tamed and turned out of their channels and led along the sides of cañons and valleys to work in mines like slaves. . . . Long will it be ere these marks are effaced, though Nature is doing what she can . . . patiently trying to heal every raw scar. (June 16, 1869; *MFS*, 73–74.)

44

Sheep, like people, are ungovernable when hungry. Excepting my guarded lily gardens, almost every leaf that these hoofed locusts can reach within a radius of a mile or two from camp has been devoured. (June 16, 1869; *MFS*, 75.)

45

Having escaped restraint, [the sheep] were, like some people we know of, afraid of their freedom, did not know what to do

with it, and seemed glad to get back into the old familiar
bondage. (June 17, 1869; *MFS*, 77.)

46

Her dress was calico rags, far from clean. In every way she
seemed sadly unlike Nature's neat well-dressed animals, though
living like them on the bounty of the wilderness. Strange that
mankind alone is dirty. (June 18, 1869; *MFS*, 78. Comment on an
Indian woman.)

47

Had she been clad in fur, or cloth woven of grass or shreddy
bark, like the juniper and libocedrus mats, she might have
seemed a rightful part of the wilderness; like a good wolf at
least, or bear. But from no point of view that I have found are
such debased fellow beings a whit more natural than the glaring
tailored tourists we saw that frightened the birds and squirrels.
(June 18, 1869; *MFS*, 78–79. Comment on an Indian woman.)

48

God himself seems to be always doing his best here, working
like a man in a glow of enthusiasm. (June 20, 1869; *Atlantic
Monthly*, February 1911, 170; *MFS*, 80.)

49

Never more, however weary, should one faint by the way
who gains the blessings of one mountain day; whatever his fate,
long life, short life, stormy or calm, he is rich forever. (June 23,
1869; *Atlantic Monthly*, February 1911, 170; *MFS*, 82.)

50

Rather weak and sickish this morning, and all about a piece
of bread. Can scarce command attention to my best studies, as
if one couldn't take a few days' saunter in the Godful woods
without maintaining a base on a wheat-field and grist-mill. Like
caged parrots we want a cracker. . . . Bread without flesh is a
good diet, as on many botanical excursions I have proved. Tea
also may easily be ignored. Just bread and water and delightful
toil is all I need. . . . (July 7, 1869; *Atlantic Monthly*, February
1911, 174; *MFS*, 103.)

51

Man seems to be the only animal whose food soils him, making much washing necessary, and shield-like bibs and napkins. (July 7, 1869; *Atlantic Monthly*, February 1911, 175; *MFS*, 104–5.)

52

We dream of bread, a sure sign we need it. (July 7, 1869; *Atlantic Monthly*, February 1911, 175; *MFS*, 106.)

53

Yet why bewail our poor inevitable ignorance? Some of the external beauty is always in sight, enough to keep every fibre of us tingling, and this we are able to gloriously enjoy though the methods of its creation may lie beyond our ken. (July 11, 1869; *MFS*, 136.)

54

We saw another party of Yosemite tourists to-day. Somehow most of these travelers seem to care but little for the glorious objects about them, though enough to spend time and money and endure long rides to see the famous valley. And when they are fairly within the mighty walls of the temple and hear the psalms of the falls, they will forget themselves and become devout. Blessed indeed should be every pilgrim in these holy mountains. (July 12, 1869; *Atlantic Monthly*, February 1911, 179; *MFS*, 138.)

55

How deathlike is sleep in this mountain air, and quick the awakening into newness of life! (July 14, 1869; *Atlantic Monthly*, February 1911, 179; *MFS*, 144.)

56

. . . a sturdy storm-enduring mountaineer of a tree, living on sunshine and snow, maintaining tough health on this diet for perhaps more than a thousand years. (July 14, 1869; *Atlantic Monthly*, February 1911, 180; *MFS*, 146. A Sierra juniper.)

57

Sheep brain must surely be poor stuff. . . . A sheep can hardly be called an animal; an entire flock is required to make one foolish individual. (July 14, 1869; *Atlantic Monthly,* February 1911, 181; *MFS,* 152.)

58

My first view of the High Sierra, first view looking down into Yosemite, the death-song of Yosemite Creek, and its flight over the vast cliff, each one of these is of itself enough for a great life-long landscape fortune—a most memorable day of days— enjoyment enough to kill if that were possible. (July 15, 1869; *Atlantic Monthly,* March 1911, 341; *MFS,* 160. On the north rim of the valley, near Yosemite Point.)

59

From form to form, beauty to beauty, ever changing, never resting, all are speeding on with love's enthusiasm, singing with the stars the eternal song of creation. (July 19, 1869; *MFS,* 169–70.)

60

Who wouldn't be a mountaineer! Up here all the world's prizes seem nothing. (July 26, 1869; *Atlantic Monthly,* March 1911, 346; *MFS,* 206.)

61

No longing for anything now or hereafter as we go home into the mountain's heart. (July 27, 1869; *MFS,* 209.)

62

No Sierra landscape that I have seen holds anything truly dead or dull, or any trace of what in manufactories is called rubbish or waste; everything is perfectly clean and pure and full of divine lessons. (July 27, 1869; *MFS,* 211.)

63

When we try to pick out anything by itself, we find it hitched to everything else in the universe. One fancies a heart like our own must be beating in every crystal and cell. . . . (July 27, 1869; *MFS,* 211.)

64

Man seems to have more difficulty in gaining food than any other of the Lord's creatures. For many in towns it is a consuming, life-long struggle; for others, the danger of coming to want is so great, the deadly habit of endless hoarding for the future is formed, which smothers all real life. . . . (August 1, 1869; *MFS*, 237–38.)

65

Reading these grand mountain manuscripts displayed through every vicissitude of heat and cold, calm and storm, upheaving volcanoes and down-grinding glaciers, we see that everything in Nature called destruction must be creation—a change from beauty to beauty. (August 21, 1869; *MFS*, 308.)

66

How lavish is Nature, building, pulling down, creating, destroying, chasing every material particle from form to form, ever changing, ever beautiful. (August 30, 1869; *Atlantic Monthly*, April 1911, 526; *MFS*, 318–19.)

67

The whole wilderness seems to be alive and familiar, full of humanity. The very stones seem talkative, sympathetic, brotherly. No wonder when we consider that we all have the same Father and Mother. (August 30, 1869; *Atlantic Monthly*, April 1911, 526; *MFS*, 319.)

68

Every day opens and closes like a flower, noiseless, effortless. Divine peace glows on all the majestic landscape, like the silent enthusiastic joy that sometimes transfigures a noble human face. (August 31, 1869; *Atlantic Monthly*, April 1911, 526; *MFS*, 319.)

69

One is constantly reminded of the infinite lavishness and fertility of Nature—inexhaustible abundance amid what seems enormous waste. And yet when we look into any of her operations that lie within reach of our minds, we learn that no particle of her material is wasted or worn out. It is eternally flowing from use to use, beauty to yet higher beauty; and we

soon cease to lament waste and death, and rather rejoice and
exult in the imperishable, unspendable wealth of the universe,
and faithfully watch and wait the reappearance of everything
that melts and fades and dies about us, feeling sure that its next
appearance will be better and more beautiful than the last.
(September 2, 1869; *MFS*, 325–26.)

70

. . . We never know where we must go, nor what guides we
are to get,—men, storms, guardian angels, or sheep. . . . Almost
everybody in the least natural is guided more than he is ever
aware of. (September 6, 1869; *Atlantic Monthly*, April 1911, 527;
MFS, 331.)

71

This I may say is the first time I have been at church in
California, led here at last, every door graciously opened for
the poor lonely worshiper. (September 7, 1869; *MFS*, 336.
Atop Cathedral Peak, the first person to climb it.)

72

Mr. Delaney . . . declares I'll be famous some day,—a kind
guess that seems strange and incredible to a wandering
wilderness lover with never a thought or dream of fame, while
humbly trying to trace and learn and enjoy Nature's lessons.
(September 9, 1869; *Atlantic Monthly*, February 1911, 527; *MFS*,
342. Delaney was the sheep-owner for whom Muir worked.)

73

Aside from mere money profit one would rather herd wolves
than sheep. (September 9, 1869; *MFS*, 343.)

Patient Observation

1869–1872

74

I am glad that the world does not miss me and that all of my days with the Lord and his works are uncounted and unmeasured. (Letter to Mrs. Carr, October 3, 1869; *LTF*, 67.)

75

I am feasting in the Lord's mountain house, and what pen may write my blessings? (Letter to Mrs. Carr, December 6, 1869; *LTF*, 71.)

76

Love of pure unblemished Nature seems to overmaster and blur out of sight all other objects and considerations. I know that I could under ordinary circumstances accumulate wealth and obtain a fair position in society, and I am arrived at an age that requires that I should choose some definite course for life. But I am sure that the mind of no truant schoolboy is more free and disengaged from all the grave plans and purposes and pursuits of ordinary orthodox life than mine. (Letter to his sister Sarah, 1869; *LAL*, vol. 1, 204.)

77

Patient observation and constant brooding above the rocks, lying upon them for years as the ice did, is the way to arrive at the truths which are graven so lavishly upon them. (Probably 1870; *JOM*, 34.)

78

Alas, how little of the world is subject to human senses!
(January 18, 1870; *JOM*, 44.)

79

These beautiful days must enrich all my life. They do not
exist as mere pictures—maps hung upon the walls of memory
to brighten at times when touched by association or will, only
to sink again like a landscape in the dark; but they saturate
themselves into every part of the body and live always.
(May 21, 1870; *JOM*, 53.)

80

All sorts of human stuff is being poured into our valley this
year, and the blank, fleshly apathy with which most of it comes
in contact with the rock and water spirits of the place is most
amazing. . . . They climb sprawlingly to their saddles like
overgrown frogs pulling themselves up a stream-bank through
the bent sedges, ride up the valley with about as much emotion
as the horses they ride upon, and comfortable when they have
"done it all," and long for the safety and flatness of their proper
homes. (Letter to Mrs. Carr, May 29, 1870; *LTF*, 80–81.)

81

. . . The tide of visitors will float slowly about the bottom of
the valley as a harmless scum, collecting in hotel and saloon
eddies, leaving the rocks and falls eloquent as ever and instinct
with imperishable beauty and greatness. (Letter to Mrs. Carr,
May 29, 1870; *LTF*, 81.)

82

The valley is full of people but they do not annoy me. I
revolve in pathless places and in higher rocks than the world
and his ribbony wife can reach. (Letter to Mrs. Carr, 1870; *LTF*,
85.)

83

The Amazon and Andes have been in all my thoughts for
many years, and I am sure that I shall meet them someday ere
I die, or become settled and civilized and useful. (Letter to Mrs.
Carr, November 4, 1870; *LAL*, vol. 1, 234.)

84

Hawthorne says that steam has spiritualized travel,
notwithstanding the smoke, friction, smells, and clatter of boat
and rail riding. This flight in a milky way of snow flowers was
the most spiritual of all my travels. . . . (*Atlantic Monthly,* April
1901, 561. This is a reference to being caught in an avalanche and
riding it down. Although this quotation might seem to be out of
place chronologically, its progenitor appeared in a letter to Mrs.
Carr, November 4, 1870, *LAL,* vol. 1, 235, as: "Hawthorne says
that steam spiritualizes travel, but I think that it squarely
degrades and materializes travel." Here Muir has taken what he
regarded as a choice passage, combined it with a later
death-threatening event, and published it thirty-one years after
he first wrote it.)

85

The astronomer looks high, the geologist low. Who looks
between on the surface of the earth? The farmer, I suppose,
but too often he sees only grain, and of that only the mere
bread-bushel-and-price of it. (1870 or 1871; *JOM,* 67.)

86

I feel sure that if you were here to see how happy I am, and
how ardently I am seeking a knowledge of the rocks you could
not call me away, but would gladly let me go with only God and
his written rocks to guide me. You would not think of calling me
to make machines or a home, or of rubbing me against other
minds, or of setting me up for measurement. (Letter to Mrs. Carr,
September 8, 1871; *LAL,* vol. 1, 293.)

87

No evil consequence from "waste of time," concerning which
good people who accomplish nothing make such a sermonizing,
has, thus far, befallen me. (September 1871; "Explorations in the
Great Tuolumne Cañon," *Overland Monthly,* August 1873, 141;
JOM, 69.)

88

The last days of this glacial winter are not yet past, so young
is our world. I used to envy the father of our race, dwelling as he
did in contact with the new-made fields and plants of Eden; but

I do so no more, because I have discovered that I also live in
"creation's dawn." The morning stars still sing together, and the
world, not yet half made, becomes more beautiful every day.
(September 1871; "Explorations in the Great Tuolumne Cañon,"
Overland Monthly, August 1873, 143; *JOM,* 72.)

89

Here was no field, nor camp, nor ruinous cabin, nor hacked
trees, nor down-trodden flowers, to disenchant the Godful
solitude. Neither did I discover here any trace or hint of lawless
forces. Among these mighty cliffs and domes there is no word
of chaos, or of desolation; every rock is as elaborately and
thoughtfully carved and finished as a crystal or shell.
(September 1871; "Explorations in the Great Tuolumne
Cañon," *Overland Monthly,* August 1873, 146; *JOM,* 76–77.)

90

No healthy man who delivers himself into the hands of
Nature can possibly doubt the doubleness of his life. Soul and
body receive separate nourishment and separate exercise, and
speedily reach a stage of development wherein each is easily
known apart from the other. Living artificially in towns, we are
sickly, and never come to know ourselves. Our torpid souls are
hopelessly entangled with our torpid bodies, and not only is
there a confused mingling of our own souls with our own
bodies, but we hardly possess a separate existence from our
neighbors. (September 1871; "Explorations in the Great
Tuolumne Cañon," *Overland Monthly,* August 1873, 146; *JOM,*
77.)

91

The life of a mountaineer is favorable to the development
of soul-life, as well as limb-life, each receiving abundance of
exercise and abundance of food. (September 1871; "Explorations
in the Great Tuolumne Cañon," *Overland Monthly,* August 1873,
146; *JOM,* 77.)

92

My legs sometimes transport me to camp, in the darkness,
over cliffs and through bogs and forests that are inaccessible to
city legs during the day. In like manner the soul sets forth upon

rambles of its own. (September 1871; "Explorations in the Great Tuolumne Cañon," *Overland Monthly*, August 1873, 146; *JOM*, 78.)

93

Toiling in the treadmills of life we hide from the lessons of Nature. We gaze morbidly through civilized fog upon our beautiful world clad with seamless beauty, and see ferocious beasts and wastes and deserts. But savage deserts and beasts and storms are expressions of God's power inseparably companioned by love. Civilized man chokes his soul as the heathen Chinese their feet. (October 1871; *JOM*, 82.)

94

Bears are made of the same dust as we, and breathe the same winds and drink of the same waters. A bear's days are warmed by the same sun, his dwellings are overdomed by the same blue sky, and his life turns and ebbs with heart-pulsings like ours, and was poured from the same First Fountain. And whether he at last goes to our stingy heaven or no, he has terrestrial immortality. His life not long, not short, knows no beginning, no ending. To him life unstinted, unplanned, is above the accidents of time, and his years, markless and boundless, equal Eternity. (October 1871; *JOM*, 82–83.)

95

Most civilized folks cry morbidness, lunacy upon all that will not weigh on Fairbank's scales or measure to that seconds rod of English brass. But we know that much that is most real will not counterpoise cast-iron, or dent our human flesh. (October 1871; **JOM,** 85.)

96

Heaven knows that John Baptist was not more eager to get all his fellow sinners into the Jordan than I to baptize all of mine in the beauty of God's mountains. (October 1871; *JOM*, 86.)

97

I am only a piece of jagged human mist drifting about these rocks & waters Heaven only knows how or wherefor. (Letter to Charles Warren Stoddard, February 20, 1872. *The Letters of Western Authors,* no. 5, May 1935.)

98

I am only a baby slowly learning my mountain alphabet. (Letter to Charles Warren Stoddard, February 20, 1872. *The Letters of Western Authors,* no. 5, May 1935.)

99

I know little of men yet I venture to say that half our best teachers are manufactured—so ground & pressed in the mills of culture that God cannot play a single tune on them. (Letter to Charles Warren Stoddard, February 20, 1872. *The Letters of Western Authors,* no. 5, May 1935.)

100

I am glad to learn my friend that you have not yet submitted yourself to any of the mouldy laws of literature. (Letter to Charles Warren Stoddard, February 20, 1872. *The Letters of Western Authors,* no. 5, May 1935.)

Nothing Goes Unrecorded

1872

101

Nothing goes unrecorded. Every word of leaf and snowflake and particle of dew . . . as well as earthquake and avalanche, is written down in Nature's book. (March 1872; *JOM*, 88.)

102

I am glad to know . . . that my unconditional surrender to Nature has produced exactly what you have foreseen—that drifting without human charts through light and dark, calm and storm, I have come to so glorious an ocean. (Letter to Mrs. Carr, March 16, 1872; *LAL*, vol. 1, 320.)

103

It is blessed to lean fully and trustingly on Nature, to experience, by taking to her a pure heart and unartificial mind, the infinite tenderness and power of her love. (Letter to Emily Pelton, April 2, 1872; *LAL*, vol. 1, 325.)

104

Compared with the intense purity and cordiality and beauty of Nature, the most delicate refinements and cultures of civilization are gross barbarisms. (Letter to Emily Pelton, April 2, 1872; *LAL*, vol. 1, 325.)

105

With reference to sight-seeing on the Pacific Coast, our
so-called trans-continental railroad is a big gun; charged with
steam and cars it belches many a tourist against the targets of the
golden State,—geysers, big trees, Yosemite . . . among which
they bump and ricochet, and rebound to their Atlantic homes,
bruised and blurred, their memories made up of a motley jam of
cascades and deserts and mountain domes, each traveler
voluntarily compacting himself into the fastest cartridge of car
and coach, as if resolved to see as little as possible. ("Rambles of
a Botanist Among the Plants and Climates of California," *Old and
New*, June 1872, 767.)

106

I am learning to live close to the lives of my friends without
ever seeing them. No miles of any measurement can separate
your soul from mine. (Letter to Mrs. Carr, August 5, 1872;
LTF, 131.)

107

This good and tough mountain-climbing flesh is not my final
home, and I'll creep out of it and fly free and grow! (August 17,
1872; *JOM*, 89.)

108

Here is a clean white-skinned glacier from the back of
McClure with glassy emerald flesh and singing crystal blood,
all bright and pure as a sky, yet handling mud and stone like a
navvy, building moraines like a plodding Irishman. (Letter to
Mrs. Carr, October 8, 1872; *LAL*, vol. 1, 345. The correct spelling
of the mountain's name is "Maclure.")

109

Here is a cascade two hundred feet wide, half a mile long,
glancing this way and that, filled with bounce and dance and
joyous hurrah, yet earnest as a tempest, and singing like angels
loose on a frolic from heaven. (Letter to Mrs. Carr, October 8,
1872; *LAL*, vol. 1, 345.)

110

There perhaps are souls that never weary, that always go
unhalting and glad, tuneful and songful as mountain water. Not
so, weary, hungry me. In all God's mountain mansions, I find no
human sympathy, and I hunger. (October 1872; *JOM*, 89.)

111

Some plants readily take on the forms and habits of society,
but generally speaking soon return to primitive simplicity, and I,
too, like a weed of cultivation feel a constant tendency to return
to primitive wildness. (October 1872; *JOM*, 90.)

112

. . . I may yet become a proper cultivated plant, cease my wild
wanderings, and form a so-called pillar or something in society,
but if so, I must, like a revived Methodist, learn to love what
I hate and to hate what I most intensely and devoutly love.
(October 1872; *JOM*, 90.)

113

I never saw one drop of blood, one red stain on all this
wilderness. Even death is in harmony here. Only in shambles
and the downy beds of homes is death terrible. (1872; *JOM*, 93.)

114

I have a low opinion of books; they are but piles of stone
set up to show coming travelers where other minds have been,
or at least signal smokes to call attention. . . . No amount of
word- making will ever make a single soul to know these
mountains. As well to seek to warm the naked and frostbitten by
lectures on caloric and pictures of flame. One day's exposure to
mountains is better than cartloads of books. See how willingly
Nature poses herself upon photographers' plates. No earthy
chemicals are so sensitive as those of the human soul. All that is
required is exposure, and purity of material. (1872; *JOM*, 94–95.)

115

. . . Anyone who has learned the language of running water
will see its character in the dark. (1872; *JOM*, 95.)

116

Some people miss flesh as a drunkard misses his dram. This depraved appetite stands greatly in the way of free days on the mountains, for meat of any kind is hard to carry, and makes a repulsive mess when jammed in a pack. . . . The butter-and-milk habit has seized most people; bread without butter or coffee without milk is an awful calamity. . . . It seems ridiculous that a man . . . should have to go beneath a cow like a calf three times a day—never weaned. (1872; *JOM*, 97.)

117

Earth has no sorrow that earth cannot heal. . . . (1872; *JOM*, 99.)

Go East, Young Man

1872–1874

118

Go east, young man, go east! Californians have only to go east a few miles to be happy. Toilers on the heat plains, toilers in the cities by the sea, whose lives are well-nigh choked by the weeds of care that have grown up and run to seed about them—leave all and go east and you cannot escape a cure for all care. (1872; *JOM*, 99.)

119

Instead of narrowing my attention to bookmaking out of material I have already eaten and drunken, I would rather stand in what all the world would call an idle manner, literally gaping with all the mouths of soul and body, demanding nothing, fearing nothing, but hoping and enjoying enormously. So-called sentimental, transcendental dreaming seems the only sensible and substantial business that one can engage in.
(January 6, 1873; *JOM*, 102–3.)

120

Drifting about among flowers and sunshine, I am like a butterfly or bee, though not half so busy or with so sure an aim. But in the midst of these methodless rovings I seek to spell out by close inspection things not well understood. Still, in the work of grave science I make but little progress.

If, in after years, I should do better in the way of exact research, then these lawless wanderings will not be without value as suggestive beginnings. But if I should be fated to walk no more with Nature, be compelled to leave all I most devoutly

love in the wilderness, return to civilization and be twisted
into the characterless cable of society, then these sweet, free,
cumberless rovings will be as chinks and slits on life's horizon,
through which I may obtain glimpses of the treasures that lie in
God's wilds beyond my reach. (January 16, 1873; *JOM,* 108.)

121

Most people who are born into the world remain babies all
their lives, their development being arrested like sun-dried
seeds. (March 1, 1873; *LAL,* vol. 1, 24.)

122

To ask me whether I could endure to live without friends is
absurd. It is easy enough to live out of material sight of friends,
but to live without human love is impossible. Quench love, and
what is left of a man's life but the folding of a few jointed bones
and square inches of flesh? Who would call that life? (March 15,
1873; *JOM,* 138.)

123

All of this big mountain bread for one day! One of the rich,
ripe days that enlarge one's life—so much of the sun upon one
side of it, so much of the moon on the other. ("A Geologist's
Winter Walk," *Overland Monthly,* April 1873, 358.)

124

Sheep are driven into Hetch Hetchy every spring, about the
same time that a nearly equal number of tourists are driven into
Yosemite; another coincident which is remarkably suggestive.
(*Boston Weekly Transcript,* March 25, 1873.)

125

We had several shocks last night. . . . 'T is most ennobling to
find that we are constructed with reference to these noble
storms, so as to draw unspeakable enjoyment from them. Are we
not rich when our six-foot column of substance sponges up
heaven above and earth beneath into its pores? Aye, we have
chambers in us the right shape for earthquakes. . . . If the human
flock . . . would go wild themselves, they would discover . . . that
the whole contents of a human soul is the whole world. (Letter to
Mrs. Carr, 1873; *LTF,* 160–61.)

126

. . . A man in his books may be said to walk the world long after he is in his grave. . . . (Late 1873; *JOM*, 168.)

127

There need be no lasting sorrow for the death of any of Nature's creations, because for every death there is always born a corresponding life. (Late 1873; *JOM*, 168.)

128

Every carpenter knows that only a dull tool will follow the grain of wood. Such a tool is the glacier, sliding with tremendous pressure past splitting precipices and smooth swelling domes, flexible as the wind, yet hard-tempered as steel. Mighty as its effects appear to us, it has only developed the predestined forms of mountain beauty which were ready and waiting to receive the baptism of light. ("Studies in the Sierra—Mountain Sculpture," *Overland Monthly*, May 1874, 403; *SIS*, 16.)

129

It would require years of enthusiastic study to master the English alphabet, if it were carved upon the flank of the Sierra in letters sixty or seventy miles long, their bases set in the foothills, their tops leaning back among the glaciers and shattered peaks of the summit, often veiled with forests and thickets, and their continuity often broken by cross-gorges and hills. ("Studies in the Sierra—Origin of Yosemite Valleys," *Overland Monthly*, June 1874, 495; *SIS*, 21.)

130

Nature is not so poor as to possess only one of anything. . . . ("Studies in the Sierra—Origin of Yosemite Valleys," *Overland Monthly*, June 1874, 496; *SIS*, 21.)

131

Every weary one seeking with damaged instinct the high founts of nature, when he chances into . . . the mountains, if accustomed to philosophize at all, if not too far gone in civilization, will ask, Whence comes? What is the secret of the mysterious enjoyment felt here—the strange calm, the divine frenzy? Whence comes the annihilation of bonds that seemed everlasting? (September 1874; *JOM*, 191.)

132

Tell me what you will of the benefactions of city civilization, of the sweet security of streets—all as part of the natural upgrowth of man towards the high destiny we hear so much of. I know that our bodies were made to thrive only in pure air, and the scenes in which pure air is found. If the death exhalations that brood the broad towns in which we so fondly compact ourselves were made visible, we should flee as from a plague. All are more or less sick; there is not a perfectly sane man in San Francisco. (September 1874; *JOM*, 191.)

133

Go now and then for fresh life. . . . Go whether or not you have faith. . . . Go up and away for life; be fleet!

I know some will heed the warning. Most will not, so full of pagan slavery is the boasted freedom of the town, and those who need rest and clean snow and sky the most will be the last to move. (September 1874; *JOM*, 191–92.)

134

Once I was let down into a deep well into which choke-damp had settled, and nearly lost my life. The deeper I was immersed into the invisible poison, the less capable I became of willing measures to escape from it. And in just this condition are those who toil or dawdle or dissipate in crowded towns, in the sinks of commerce or pleasure. (September 1874; *JOM*, 192.)

135

When I first came down to the city from my mountain home, I began to wither, and wish instinctively for the vital woods and high sky. Yet I lingered month after month, plodding at `duty.' At length I chanced to see a lovely goldenrod in bloom in a weedy spot alongside one of the less frequented sidewalks there. Suddenly I was aware of the ending of summer and fled. Then, once away, I saw how shrunken and lean I was, and how glad I was I had gone. (September 1874; *JOM*, 192.)

136

The freedom I felt was exhilarating, and the burning heat, and thirst, and faintness could not make it less. Before I had walked ten miles, I was wearied and footsore, but it was real earnest work and I liked it. Any kind of simple, natural destruction is preferable to the numb, dumb apathetic deaths of a town. (Letter to Mrs. Carr, September 1874; *The Craftsman*, March 1905, 658; LAL, vol. 2, 13.)

137

. . . I gave heed to the confiding stream, mingled freely with the flowers and light, and shared in the confidence of their exceeding peace. ("By-Ways of Yosemite Travel. Bloody Cañon," *Overland Monthly*, September 1874, 273.)

138

I never believed the doctrine of deserts, whether as applied to mountains or men. Nature's love is universal. . . . ("By-Ways of Yosemite Travel. Bloody Cañon," *Overland Monthly*, September 1874, 273.)

139

The older faces were strangely blurred and abraded, and sectioned off by a kind of cleavage points, as if they had laid castaway on the mountains for ages. Viewed at a little distance, they formed mere dirt-specks in the landscape, and I was glad to see them fade out of sight. ("By-Ways of Yosemite Travel. Bloody Cañon," *Overland Monthly*, September 1874, 272; *Scribner's Monthly*, March 1879, 650; *Picturesque California*, 29. Muir's first encounter with Mono Indians, at Mono Pass, 1869. The wording varied from one version to another.)

140

. . . I met the Arctic daisies, in all their perfection of purity and spirituality; gentle mountaineers, face to face with the sky, kept safe and warm by a thousand miracles. ("By-Ways of Yosemite Travel. Bloody Cañon," *Overland Monthly*, September 1874, 272; *Scribner's Monthly*, March 1879, 651; *Picturesque California*, 29.)

141

Civilization and fever and all the morbidness that has been hooted at me have not dimmed my glacial eye, and I care to live only to entice people to look at Nature's loveliness. (Letter to Mrs. Carr, October 7, 1874; *LAL,* vol. 2, 29.)

142

We little know how much wildness there is in us. Only a few generations separate us from our grandfathers that were savage as wolves. This is the secret of our love for the hunt. Savageness is natural, civilization is strained and unnatural. It required centuries to tame men as we find them, but if turned loose they would return to killing and bloody barbarism in as many years. (November 1874; *JOM,* 199.)

143

When Nature lifted the ice-sheet from the mountains, she may well be said, not to have turned a new leaf, but to have made a new one from the old. ("Studies in the Sierra—Post-Glacial Denudation," *Overland Monthly,* November 1874, 393; *SIS,* 62.)

144

. . . Every soil-atom seems to yield enthusiastic obedience to law—bowlders and mud-grains moving to music as harmoniously as the far-whirling planets. ("Studies in the Sierra—Formation of Soils," *Overland Monthly,* December 1874, 540; *SIS,* 88.)

Nature is a Good Mother

1875–1877

145

Moral improvers have calls to preach. I have a friend who has a call to plow, and woe to the daisy sod or azalea thicket that falls under the savage redemption of his keen steel shares. Not content with the so-called subjugation of every terrestrial bog, rock, and moor-land, he would fain discover some method of reclamation applicable to the ocean and the sky, that in due calendar time they might be made to bud and blossom as the rose. ("Wild Wool," *Overland Monthly*, April 1875, 361; *STT*, 3. "The desert shall rejoice, and blossom as the rose." *Isaiah* 35:1.)

146

. . . The barbarous notion is almost universally entertained by civilized men, that there is in all the manufactures of nature something essentially coarse which can and must be eradicated by human culture. ("Wild Wool," *Overland Monthly*, April 1875, 361; *STT*, 4.)

147

Nature is a good mother, and sees well to the clothing of her many bairns—birds with smoothly imbricated feathers, beetles with shining jackets, and bears with shaggy furs. ("Wild Wool," *Overland Monthly*, April 1875, 361–62; *STT*, 5.)

148

To obtain a hearing on behalf of nature from any other stand-point than that of human use is almost impossible. Domestic flocks yield more flannel per sheep than the wild, therefore it is claimed that culture has improved upon wildness; and so it has as far as flannel is concerned, but all to the contrary as far as a sheep's dress is concerned. ("Wild Wool," *Overland Monthly*, April 1875, 363; *STT*, 11.)

149

No dogma taught by the present civilization seems to form so insuperable an obstacle in the way of a right understanding of the relations which culture sustains as to wildness, as that which declares that the world was made especially for the uses of men. Every animal, plant, and crystal controverts it in the plainest terms. Yet it is taught from century to century as something ever new and precious, and in the resulting darkness the enormous conceit is allowed to go unchallenged. ("Wild Wool," *Overland Monthly*, April 1875, 364; *STT*, 11–12.)

150

I have never yet happened upon a trace of evidence . . . to show that any one animal was ever made for another as much as it was made for itself. ("Wild Wool," *Overland Monthly*, April 1875, 364; *STT*, 12.)

151

. . . We are governed more than we know, and most when we are wildest. Plants, animals, and stars are all kept in place, bridled along appointed ways, with one another, and through the midst of one another—killing and being killed, eating and being eaten, in harmonious proportions and quantities. . . . Stars attract each other as they are able, and harmony results. Wild lambs eat as many wild flowers as they can find or desire, and men and wolves eat the lambs to just the same extent. ("Wild Wool," *Overland Monthly*, April 1875, 364; *STT*, 13.)

152

. . . We take wild sheep home and subject them to the many extended processes of husbandry, and finish by cooking them in a cooking pot—a process which completes all sheep improvements as far as man is concerned. ("Wild Wool," *Overland Monthly*, 365; *STT*, 14.)

153

Now the architecture of the forest is seen in all its grandeur.
In the daylight we see too much. . . . But at night all is massed,
and the spires and towers of black shoot up to the gray sky
along the meadow, forming a wall, a street of trees.
(August 1875; *JOM*, 212.)

154

We read our Bibles and remain fearful and uncomfortable
amid Nature's loving destructions, her beautiful deaths. Talk of
immortality! After a whole day in the woods, we are already
immortal. When is the end of such a day? (August 1875; *JOM*,
213.)

155

Here it is six or seven thousand feet above the sea, yet in all
that tranquil scene we feel no remoteness, no rest from care and
chafing duties because here they have no existence. Every sense
is satisfied. For us there is no past, no future. We live in the
present and are full. No room for hungry hopes, none for regrets,
none for exultation, none for fear. (August 1875; *JOM*, 214.)

156

I often wonder what man will do with the mountains—that is,
with their utilizable, destructible garments. Will he cut down all
the trees to make ships and houses? If so, what will be the final
and far upshot? Will human destructions like those of Nature—
fire and flood and avalanche—work out a higher good, a finer
beauty? Will a better civilization come in accord with obvious
nature, and all this wild beauty be set to human poetry and
song? Another universal outpouring of lava, or the coming of a
glacial period, could scarce wipe out the flowers and shrubs
more effectively than do the sheep. And what then is coming?
What is the human part of the mountains' destiny? (August 1875;
JOM, 215.)

157

One can make a day of any size, and regulate the rising
and setting of his own sun and the brightness of its shining.
(August 1875; *JOM*, 218.)

158

The woods are made for the wise and strong. In their very essence they are the counterparts of man. Their beauty—all their forms and voices and scents—seem, as they really are, reminiscences of something already experienced. . . . Let an imprisoned man see the grand woods for the first time . . . he will enjoy their beauty and feel their fitness as if he had learned of them from childhood. (August 1875; *JOM*, 220.)

159

Our crude civilization engenders a multitude of wants, and lawgivers are ever at their wits' end devising. The hall and the theater and the church have been invented, and compulsory education. Why not compulsory recreation? Our forefathers forged chains of duty and habit, which bind us not withstanding our boasted freedom, and we ourselves in desperation add link to link, groaning and making medicinal laws for relief. Yet few think of pure rest or of the healing power of Nature. How hard to pull or shake people out of town! Earthquakes cannot do it, nor even plagues. These only cause the civilized to pray and ring bells and cower in corners of bedrooms and churches. (November 12, 1875; *JOM*, 234.)

160

Mass-saying is not so generally developed in connection with natural wonders as dancing. Thus one of the first conceits excited by the giant sequoias was a dance on the stump of the largest. We also have seen dancing over Niagara; dancing in the famous Bower Cave above Coulterville; and in no place of an equal number of inhabitants have I seen so much dancing as in Yosemite. A dance on the hitherto inaccessible South Dome will undoubtedly follow the completion of the ladders. ("Summering in the Sierra," *San Francisco Daily Evening Bulletin,* August 12, 1876; *MOC,* 335. "South Dome" was an early name for Half Dome.)

161

The regular tourist, ever on the flow, is one of the most characteristic productions of the present century; and however frivolous and inappreciative the poorer specimens may appear, viewed comprehensively they are a most hopeful and significant sign of the times, indicating at least the beginning of our return to nature,—for going to the mountains is going home. . . . Men, women and children of every creed and color come here from every nation; manly, hard-fisted farmers from the old West, shrewd business men, builders, lawyers, doctors, and "divines;" scientists seeking causes; wealthy and elegant loafers trying to escape from themselves; the so-called high and low, titled and obscure, all in some degree seeing and loving fresh, wild beauty, and traveling to better purpose than they know, borne onward like ships at sea by currents they cannot understand. ("Summering in the Sierra," *San Francisco Daily Evening Bulletin,* August 24, 1876; *Picturesque California,* 59.)

162
. . . Unfortunately, man is in the woods, and waste and pure destruction are already making rapid headway. ("On the Post-Glacial History of Sequoia Gigantea," *Proceedings of the American Association for the Advancement of Science,* May 1877, 252; *MOC,* 198.)

163
. . . Strange as it must seem to Gentiles, the many wives of one man, instead of being repelled from one another by natural jealousy, appear to be drawn all the closer together, as if the real marriage existed between the wives only. Groups of half a dozen or so may frequently be seen on the streets in close conversation, looking as innocent and unspeculative, as a lot of heifers, while the masculine saints pass them by as if they belonged to a distinct species. In the Tabernacle last Sunday, one of the elders of the church, in discoursing upon the good things in life, the possessions of Latter Day Saints, enumerated fruitful fields, horses, cows, wives, and implements; the wives being placed as above, between the cows and implements, without receiving any superior emphasis. ("City of the Saints," *San Francisco Daily Evening Bulletin,* May 22, 1877; *STT,* 110.)

164
An hour's ride over stretches of bare, brown plain, and through corn-fields and orange groves, brought me to the

handsome, conceited little town of Los Angeles, where one finds
Spanish adobes and Yankee shingles meeting and overlapping in
very curious antagonism. ("Semi-Tropical California," *San
Francisco Daily Evening Bulletin,* September 7, 1877; *STT,* 136–37.)

165

When a man plants a tree he plants himself. Every root is an
anchor, over which he rests with grateful interest, and becomes
sufficiently calm to feel the joy of living. ("Semi-Tropical
California," *San Francisco Daily Evening Bulletin,* September 7,
1877; *STT,* 141.)

166

It is seldom that I experience much difficulty in leaving
civilization for God's wilds. . . . (Letter to Gen. John Bidwell,
October 10, 1877; *LAL,* 73.)

Gold and Glaciers

1878–1888

167

Most men . . . whether savage or civilized, become apathetic toward all plants that have no other apparent use than the use of beauty. ("The Humming-Bird of the California Water-Falls," *Scribner's Monthly*, February 1878, 553; *MOC*, 295.)

168

The great, rousing, fragrant fire is the very god of the house. No wonder the old nations with their fresher instincts had their fireside gods. A fine place this to forget weariness and wrongs and bad business. ("Tahoe in Winter," *San Francisco Daily Evening Bulletin*, April 3, 1878.)

169

. . . Nevada is beautiful in her wildness, and if tillers of the soil can thus be brought to see that possibly Nature may have other uses even for rich soil besides the feeding of human beings, then will these foodless "deserts" have taught a fine lesson. ("Nevada Farms," *San Francisco Daily Evening Bulletin*, October 5, 1878.)

170

Winds are advertisements of all they touch . . . telling their wanderings even by their scents alone. ("A Wind Storm in the Forests of the Yuba," *Scribner's Monthly*, November 1878, 59; *MOC*, 254.)

171

We all travel the milky way together, trees and men. . . . Trees are travelers, in the ordinary sense. They make many journeys,

not extensive ones, it is true; but our own little comes and goes
are only little more than tree-wavings—many of them not so
much. ("A Wind Storm in the Forests of the Yuba," *Scribner's
Monthly*, November 1878, 59; *MOC*, 256.)

172

The Merced River . . . is remarkably like an elm-tree, and it
requires but little effort on the part of the imagination to picture
it standing upright, with all its lakes hanging upon its spreading
branches, the topmost eighty miles in height. ("The Mountain
Lakes of California," *Scribner's Monthly*, January 1879, 412;
MOC, 102.)

173

The healthful ministry of wealth is blessed; and surely it is a
fine thing that so many are so eager to find the gold and silver
that lies hid in the veins of the mountains. But in the search the
seekers too often become insane, and strike about blindly in the
dark like raving madmen. ("Nevada's Dead Towns," *San
Francisco Daily Evening Bulletin*, January 15, 1879; *STT*, 200.)

174

. . . Drifts and tunnels in the rocks may perhaps be regarded
as the prayers of the prospector, offered for the wealth he so
earnestly craves. But like prayers of any kind not in harmony
with nature, they are unanswered.

But after all, effort however misapplied, is better than
stagnation. Better toil blindly, beating every stone in turn for
grains of gold, whether they contain any or not, than lie waste
in apathetic decay. ("Nevada's Dead Towns," *San Francisco
Daily Evening Bulletin*, January 15, 1879; *San Francisco Examiner*,
August 23, 1897.)

175

The streets here are barren and beeless and ineffably muddy
and mean-looking. How people can keep hold of the conceptions
of New Jerusalem and immortality of souls with so much mud
and gutter, is to me admirably strange. A Eucalyptus bush
on every other corner, standing tied to a painted stick, and a
geranium sprout in a pot on every tenth window sill may
help heavenward a little, but how little amid so muckle

down-dragging mud! (Letter to Dr. and Mrs. John Strentzel from
San Francisco, January 28, 1879; *LAL,* vol. 2, 118.)

176

. . . I was familiar with storms, and enjoyed them, knowing
well that in right relations with them they are ever kindly.
(The trip of 1879. "The Discovery of Glacier Bay," *Century
Magazine,* June 1895, 234.)

177

As we sat by the camp-fire the brightness of the sky brought
on a long talk with the Indians about the stars; and their eager,
childlike attention was refreshing to see as compared with the
decent, deathlike apathy of weary civilized people, in whom
natural curiosity has been quenched in toil and care and poor,
shallow comfort. (The trip of 1879. "The Discovery of Glacier
Bay," *Century Magazine,* June 1895, 240.)

178

. . . The glacier flowed over its ground as a river flows over
a boulder; and since it emerged from the icy sea as from a
sepulcher it has been sorely beaten with storms; but from all
those deadly, crushing, bitter experiences comes this delicate life
and beauty, to teach us that what we in our faithless ignorance
and fear call destruction is creation. (The trip of 1880. "The
Discovery of Glacier Bay," *Century Magazine,* June 1895, 244–45.)

As an example of how Muir reworked his earlier prose, the
following passage is from page 267 of Travels in Alaska,
published in 1915, the year after Muir's death: ". . . Out of all the
cold darkness and glacial crushing and grinding comes this
warm, abounding beauty and life to teach us that what we in our
faithless ignorance and fear call destruction is creation finer
and finer."

179

. . . How wonderful it seems that ice formed from pressed
snow on the far-off mountains two or three hundred years ago
should still be pure and lovely in color, after all its travel and toil
in the rough mountain quarries in grinding and fashioning the
face of the coming landscape! (The trip of 1880. "The Discovery
of Glacier Bay," *Century Magazine,* June 1895, 247. A differently

worded version of this appeared earlier in "Alaska," Alaska via
Northern Pacific R.R., Northern Pacific Railroad, 1891, 13.)

180

Go where we will, all over the world, we seem to have been
there before. ("Alaska Glaciers," *San Francisco Daily Evening
Bulletin,* September 23, 1879; *TIA,* 61.)

181

. . . One learns that the world, though made, is yet being
made. That this is still the morning of creation. That mountains,
long conceived, are now being born, brought to light by the
glaciers, channels traced for rivers, basins hollowed for lakes.
That moraine soil is being ground and outspread for coming
plants . . . while the finest part of the grist, seen hastening far
out to sea, is being stored away in the darkness, and builded,
particle on particle, cementing and crystallizing, to make the
mountains and valleys and plains of other landscapes, which,
like fluent pulsing water, rise and fall, and pass on through the
ages in endless rhythm and beauty. ("Alaska Glaciers," *San
Francisco Daily Evening Bulletin,* September 27, 1879; *TIA,* 67–68.)

182

Wherever you chance to be always seems at the moment of
all places the best; and you feel that there can be no happiness in
this world or in any other for those who may not be happy here.
("Wanderings in Alaska," *San Francisco Daily Evening Bulletin,*
November 1, 1879; *TIA,* 69.)

183

The chief promised to pray like a white man every morning,
and to bury the dead as the whites do. "I often wondered," he
said, "where the dead went to. Now I am glad to know." (The
trip of 1879. *TIA,* 162. An Indian chief at a Hoona village on
Chicagof Island.)

184

Mr. Young was eager for news. I told him there could be no
news of importance about a town. We only had real news, drawn
from the wilderness. (The return to Wrangell Island in 1879. *TIA,*
195.)

185

. . . There is in some minds a tendency toward a wrong love of the marvelous and mysterious, which leads to the belief that whatever is remote must be better than what is near. ("Alaska Gold Fields," *San Francisco Daily Evening Bulletin*, January 10, 1880; revised version in the *San Francisco Examiner*, October 11, 1897.)

186

Now, in the deep, brooding silence all seems motionless, as if the work of creation were done. But in the midst of this outer steadfastness we know there is incessant motion. Ever and anon, avalanches are falling from yonder peaks. These cliff-bound glaciers seemingly wedged and immovable, are flowing like water and grinding the rocks beneath them. The lakes are lapping their granite shores and wearing them away, and every one of these rills and young rivers is fretting the air into music, and carrying the mountains to the plains. Here are the roots of all the life of the lowlands with all their wealth of vineyard and grove, and here more simply than elsewhere is the eternal flux of nature manifested. (Muir atop Mount Ritter, the first ascent, October 1872. "In the Heart of the California Alps," *Scribner's Monthly*, July 1880, 351; *Picturesque California*, 18; a truncated version in *MOC*, 69.)

187

Jagged-toothed wolves and wildcats harmonize smoothly enough, but engines for the destruction of human beings are only devilish, though they carry preachers and prayers and open up views of sad, scant tears. (Letter to his wife, August 2, 1880; *LAL*, vol. 2, 141. From aboard ship off Cape Flattery, Washington, tied up next to a British ironclad.)

188

How thick a mass of sound, serviceable ignorance is comfortably covered up in the stupid word instinct! Simply by pronouncing this one fetish word, all the wisdom, all the mental powers of animals, lose their natural significance, are at once emptied. (August 30, 1880; *JOM*, 278. Memories of the dog Stickeen.)

189

Glaciers, back in their cold solitudes, work apart from men, exerting their tremendous energies in silence and darkness. Outspread, spirit-like, they brood above the predestined landscapes, work on unwearied through immeasurable ages, until, in the fullness of time, the mountains and valleys are brought forth, channels furrowed for the rivers, basins made for the lakes and meadows, and long, deep arms of the sea, soils spread for the forests and the fields—then they shrink and vanish like summer clouds. ("The Ancient Glaciers of the Sierra," *The Californian*, December 1880, 557; *YOS*, 194–95.)

190

They had a few poles for the frame of a boat and skins to cover it, and for food a piece of walrus flesh which they ate raw. This, with a gun and a few odds and ends, was all their property, yet they seemed more confident of their ability to earn a living than most whites on their farms. (May 31, 1881; *COC*, 30. Eskimos from a village on St. Lawrence Island, Alaska.)

191

A few snow crystals were shaken down from a black cloud towards midnight, but most of the day was one of deep peace, in which God's love was manifest as in a countenance. ("At St. Michael's," *San Francisco Daily Evening Bulletin*, August 16, 1881; *COC*, 80.)

192

. . . The rocks where the exposure to storms is greatest are all the more lavishly clothed upon with beauty—beauty growing with and depending upon the violence of the gale. ("At East Cape," *San Francisco Daily Evening Bulletin*, August 16, 1881. A considerably revised version is in *COC*, 104: ". . . The rocks where the exposure to storms is the greatest, and where only ruin seems to be the object, are all the more lavishly clothed upon with beauty. . . . In like manner do men find themselves enriched by storms that seem only big with ruin.")

193

A little schooner has a boat out in the edge of the pack killing walruses. . . . A puff of smoke now and then, a dull report, and a

huge animal rears and falls—another, and another, as they lie
on the ice without showing any alarm, waiting to be killed, like
cattle lying in a barnyard!

. . . In nothing does man, with his grand notions of heaven
and charity, show forth his innate, low-bred, wild animalism
more clearly than in his treatment of his brother beasts. From
the shepherd with his lambs to the red-handed hunter, it is the
same; no recognition of rights—only murder in one form or
another. (July 23, 1881; *COC*, 142–43.)

194

. . . How civilized people, seeking for heavens and angels
and millenniums, and the reign of universal peace and love, can
enjoy this red, brutal amusement, is not so easily accounted for.
Such soft, fuzzy, sentimental aspirations, and the frame of mind
that can reap giggling, jolly pleasure from the blood and agony
and death of these fine animals, with their humanlike groans,
are too devilish for anything but hell. Of all the animals man is
at once the worst and the best. (August 2, 1881; *COC*, 162.
Hunters killing polar bears from the deck of the Corwin.)

195

This species [silver pine] . . . gives forth the finest music to
the wind. . . . I think I could approximate to my position on the
mountains by this pine-music alone. If you would catch the
tones of separate needles, climb a tree. ("The Coniferous Forests
of the Sierra Nevada," *Scribner's Monthly*, September 1881, 721;
MOC, 167.)

196

. . . No portion of the world is so barren as not to yield a rich
and precious harvest of divine truth. ("Out of the Arctic," *San
Francisco Daily Evening Bulletin*, October 25, 1881; *COC*, 204.)

197

Only by going alone in silence, without baggage, can one
truly get into the heart of the wilderness. All other travel is mere
dust and hotels and baggage and chatter. (Letter to his wife, July
1888; *LAL*, vol. 2, 245.)

198

One must labor for beauty as for bread here as elsewhere.
("The Yosemite Valley," *Picturesque California*, 63; *YOS*, 28.)

199

... By forces seemingly antagonistic and destructive Nature
accomplishes her beneficent designs—now a flood of fire, now
a flood of ice, now a flood of water; and again in the fullness of
time an outburst of organic life.... ("Mt. Shasta," *Picturesque
California*, 148; *STT*, 36.)

200

It is not long since we all were cave-men and followed game
for food as truly as wildcat or wolf, and the long repression of
civilization seems to make the rebound to savage love of blood
all the more violent. This frenzy, fortunately, does not last long
in its most exaggerated form, and after a season of wildness
refined gentlemen from cities are not more cruel than hunters
and trappers who kill for a living. ("Mt. Shasta," *Picturesque
California*, 151–52; *STT*, 45.)

Tourists and Development

1888

201

Now that the railroad has been built up the Sacramento, everybody with money may go to Mount Shasta, the weak as well as the strong, fine-grained, succulent people whose legs have never ripened as well as sinewy mountaineers seasoned long in the weather. This, surely, is not the best way of going to the mountains, yet it is better than staying below. Many still small voices will not be heard in the noisy rush and din, suggestive of going to the sky in a chariot of fire or a whirlwind, as one is shot up to the Shasta-mark in a booming palace-car cartridge; up the rocky cañon, skimming the foaming river, above the level reaches, above the dashing spray—fine exhilarating translation, yet a pity to go so fast in a blur where so much might be seen and enjoyed. (1888; "Mt. Shasta," *Picturesque California*, 152; *STT*, 46–47.)

202

The mountains are fountains not only of rivers and fertile soils, but of men. Therefore we are all, in some sense, mountaineers, and going to the mountains is going home. Yet how many are doomed to toil in town shadows while the white mountains beckon all along the horizon! (1888; "Mt. Shasta," *Picturesque California*, 152; *STT*, 47.)

203

Up the cañon to Shasta should be a cure for all care. But many
on arrival seem at a loss to know what to do with themselves,
and seek shelter in the hotel, as if that were the Shasta they
had come for. Others never leave the rail, content with the
window-view, and cling to the comforts of the sleeping-car
like blind mice to their mothers. Many are sick and have been
dragged to the healing wilderness unwillingly for body-good
alone. Were the parts of the human machine detachable like
Yankee inventions, how strange would be the gatherings on the
mountains of pieces of people out of repair! (1888; "Mt. Shasta,"
Picturesque California, 152; *STT*, 47–48.)

204

Up the mountain they go, high-heeled and high-hatted, laden
like Christian with mortifications and mortgages of divers sorts
and degrees, some suffering from the sting of bad bargains,
others exulting in good ones. . . . (1888; "Mt. Shasta," *Picturesque
California*, 153; *STT*, 48.)

205

None may wholly escape the good of Nature, however
imperfectly exposed to her blessings. The minister will not
preach a perfectly flat and sedimentary sermon after climbing .
a snowy peak; and the fair play and tremendous impartiality
of Nature, so tellingly displayed, will surely affect the after
pleadings of the lawyer. Fresh air at least will get into
everybody, and the cares of mere business will be quenched like
the fires of a sinking ship. (1888; "Mt. Shasta," *Picturesque
California*, 153; *STT*, 48.)

206

Going in noisy groups, and with guns so shining, they are
oftentimes confronted by inquisitive Douglass squirrels, and are
thus given opportunities for shooting; but the larger animals
retire at their approach and seldom are seen. Other gun-people,
too wise or too lifeless to make much noise, move slowly along
the trails and about the open spots of the woods like benumbed
beetles in a snow-drift. Such hunters are themselves hunted by

the animals, which in perfect safety follow them out of curiosity. (1888; "Mt. Shasta," *Picturesque California*, 153; *STT*, 50.)

207

Well I know the weariness of snow-climbing, and the frosts, and the dangers of mountaineering so late in the year; therefore I could not ask a guide to go with me, even had one been willing. (1888; "Mt. Shasta," *Picturesque California*, 157; *STT*, 59–60.)

208

Perhaps the profession of doing good may be full, but everybody should be kind at least to himself. Take a course in good water and air, and in the eternal youth of Nature you may renew your own. Go quietly, alone; no harm will befall you. Some have strange, morbid fears as soon as they find themselves with Nature even in the kindest and wildest of her solitudes, like very sick children afraid of their mother—as if God were dead and the devil were King. (1888; "Mt. Shasta," *Picturesque California*, 165; *STT*, 82.)

209

The great wilds of our country once held to be boundless and inexhaustible are being rapidly invaded and overrun in every direction, and everything destructible in them is being destroyed. How far destruction may go is not easy to guess. Every landscape low and high seems doomed to be trampled and harried. (1888; "Mt. Shasta," *Picturesque California*, 173–74; *STT*, 104.)

210

The wedges of development are being driven hard and none of the obstacles or defenses of nature can long withstand the onset of this immeasurable industry. (1888; "Washington and Puget Sound," *Picturesque California*, 265; *STT*, 205. A reference to the timber and mining industries.)

211

The view we enjoyed from the summit could hardly be surpassed in sublimity and grandeur; but one feels far from home so high in the sky. . . . More pleasure is to be found at the foot of mountains than on their frozen tops. Doubly happy, however, is the man to whom lofty mountain tops are within reach, for the lights that shine there illumine all that lies below. (1888; "Washington and Puget Sound," *Picturesque California,* 288; *STT,* 269–70.)

212

The whole mountain appeared as one glorious manifestation of divine power, enthusiastic and benevolent, glowing like a countenance with ineffable repose and beauty before which we could only gaze in devout and lowly admiration. (1888; "The Basin of the Columbia River," *Picturesque California,* 395; *STT,* 297.)

213

Most travelers content themselves with what they may chance to see from car-windows, hotel verandas, or the deck of a steamer on the Lower Columbia; clinging to the battered highways like drowning sailors to a life-raft. When an excursion into the woods is proposed, all sorts of exaggerated or imaginary dangers are conjured up, filling the kindly, soothing wilderness with colds, fevers, Indians, bears, snakes, bugs, impassable rivers, and jungles of brush, to which is always added quick and sure starvation. (1888; "The Basin of the Columbia River," *Picturesque California,* 401; *STT,* 312.)

214

. . . There was very little danger to be met in passing through this wilderness as far as animals were concerned, and but little of any kind as compared with the dangers encountered in crowded houses and streets. (1888; "The Basin of the Columbia River," *Picturesque California,* 402; *STT,* 314.)

215

Used, wasted, canned and sent in shiploads to all the world, a grand harvest was reaped every year while nobody sowed. (1888; "The Basin of the Columbia River," *Picturesque California,* 413; *STT,* 344. A reference to the salmon industry.)

The Range of Light

1889–1897

216

At present the valley is like a grand hall, its walls covered with fine paintings and perfect in every way, and the floor covered with a beautiful carpet, but torn and dusty in some spots, and strewn with unsightly litter. The stench of a certain pig sty rises to the top of the domes at least, and a train of cars might be loaded with tin cans and other kitchen-midden rubbish, lying exposed in this pleasure ground of the world where everyone may see it, as if like precious silverware it were exposed for sale. ("Yosemite Valley," *San Francisco Daily Evening Bulletin,* June 21, 1889.)

217

If possible and profitable every tree, bush and leaf, with the soil they are growing on, and the whole solid uplift of the mountains would be cut, blasted, scraped, shoveled and shipped away to any market home or foreign. Everything without exception, even to souls and geography, would be sold for money could a market be found for such articles. ("Forests of the Sierra," *San Francisco Daily Evening Bulletin,* June 29, 1889.)

218

All the basins draining into Yosemite are really a part of the valley, as their streams are a part of the Merced. Cut off from its branches, Yosemite is only a stump. However gnarly and picturesque, no tree that is beheaded looks well. But like ants creeping in the furrows of the bark, few of all the visitors to the Valley see more than the stump, and but little of that. To preserve the Valley and leave all its related rocks, waters, forests, to fire and sheep and lumbermen is like keeping the grand hall of entrance of a palace for royalty, while all the other apartments from cellar to dome are given up to the common or uncommon use of industry—butcher-shops, vegetable-stalls, liquor-saloons, lumber-yards.

. . . The one main hall has a hog-pen in the middle of the floor, and the whole concern seems hopeless as far as the destruction and desecration can go. Some of that stink, I'm afraid, has got into the pores of the rocks even. Perhaps it was the oncoming shadow of this desecration that caused the great flood and earthquake. . . . (Letter to Robert Underwood Johnson, March 4, 1890; *LAL*, vol. 2, 239.)

219

. . . A man who neither believed in God nor glaciers must be very bad, indeed the worst of all unbelievers. (The trip of 1890, in camp at Glacier Bay. *TIA*, 274.)

220

Most people who travel look only at what they are directed to look at. Great is the power of the guidebook-maker, however ignorant. (The trip of 1890, in camp at Glacier Bay. *TIA*, 276.)

221

All the wide world is beautiful, and it matters but little where we go. . . . The spot where we chance to be always seems the best. . . . (The Alaska trip, June 1890. *JOM*, 299.)

222

. . . Some of the days I have spent alone in the depths of the wilderness have shown me that immortal life beyond the grave is not essential to perfect happiness. . . . (The Alaska trip, June 1890. *JOM*, 301.)

223

Storms are never counted among the resources of a country, yet how far they go towards making brave people. No rush, no corrupting sloth among people who are called to cope with storms with faces set. . . . (The Alaska trip, June 1890. *JOM*, 312.)

224

I never saw a discontented tree. They grip the ground as
though they liked it, and though fast rooted they travel about
as far as we do. (The Alaska trip, July 1890. *JOM*, 313.)

225

The clearest way into the Universe is through a forest
wilderness. (The Alaska trip, July 1890. *JOM*, 313.)

226

This is one of the still, hushed, ripe days when we fancy we
might hear the beating of Nature's heart. (The Alaska trip, July
1890. *JOM*, 314.)

227

In God's wildness lies the hope of the world—the great fresh
unblighted, unredeemed wilderness. The galling harness of
civilization drops off, and the wounds heal ere we are aware.
(The Alaska trip, July 1890. *JOM*, 317.)

228

Most people are on the world, not in it—have no conscious
sympathy or relationship to anything about them—undiffused,
separate, and rigidly alone like marbles of polished stone,
touching but separate. (The Alaska trip, July 1890. *JOM*, 320.)

229

Then it seemed to me the Sierra should be called, not
the Nevada, or Snowy Range, but the Range of Light.
("The Treasures of the Yosemite," *Century Magazine*,
August 1890, 483; *MOC*, 3.)

230

. . . Nature chose for a tool not the earthquake or lightning
to rend and split asunder, nor the stormy torrent or eroding
rain, but the tender snow-flowers noiselessly falling through
unnumbered centuries, the offspring of the sun and sea.
(1894; *MOC*, 16.)

231

Accidents in the mountains are less common than in the
lowlands, and these mountain mansions are decent, delightful,

even divine, places to die in, compared with the doleful
chambers of civilization. Few places in this world are more
dangerous than home. Fear not, therefore, to try the
mountain-passes. They will kill care, save you from deadly
apathy, set you free, and call forth every faculty into vigorous,
enthusiastic action. Even the sick should try these so-called
dangerous passes, because for every unfortunate they kill, they
cure a thousand. (1894; *MOC,* 79.)

232

No other tree in the world . . . has looked down on so
many centuries as the Sequoia, or opens such impressive
and suggestive views into history. (1894; *MOC,* 182.)

233

The very first reservation that ever was made in this world
had the same fate. That reservation was very moderate in its
dimensions and the boundaries were run by the Lord himself.
That reservation contained only one tree—the smallest
reservation that ever was made. Yet, no sooner was it made
than it was attacked by everybody in the world—the devil,
one woman and one man. This has been the history of every
reservation that has been made since that time; that is, as soon as
a reservation is once created then the thieves and the devil and
his relations come forward to attack it. ("Muir on Caminetti's
Bill," *San Francisco Daily Evening Bulletin,* January 15, 1895. The
bill proposed to reduce the size of Yosemite National Park by
half, and to open the area to lumbering and grazing.)

234

Nature is always lovely, invincible, glad, whatever is done
and suffered by her creatures. All scars she heals, whether in
rocks or water or sky or hearts. (March 24, 1895; *JOM,* 337.)

235

Government protection should be thrown around every wild
grove and forest on the mountains, as it is around every private
orchard, and the trees in public parks. To say nothing of their
value as fountains of timber, they are worth infinitely more than
all the gardens and parks of town. (1895; *JOM,* 350–51.)

236

No matter into what depths of degradation humanity may sink, I will never despair while the lowest love the pure and the beautiful and know it when they see it. (1895; *JOM*, 353.)

237

The battle we have fought, and are still fighting . . . is a part of the eternal conflict between right and wrong, and we cannot expect to see the end of it. ("The National Parks and Forest Reservations," *Sierra Club Bulletin,* January 1896, 276.)

238

. . . I doubt not, if only one of our grand trees on the Sierra were reserved as an example and type of all that is most noble and glorious in mountain trees, it would not be long before you would find a lumberman and a lawyer at the foot of it, eagerly proving by every law terrestrial and celestial that that tree must come down. ("The National Parks and Forest Reservations," *Sierra Club Bulletin,* January 1896, 276.)

239

Few are altogether deaf to the preaching of pine trees. Their sermons on the mountains go to our hearts; and if people in general could be got into the woods, even for once, to hear the trees speak for themselves, all difficulties in the way of forest preservation would vanish. ("The National Parks and Forest Reservations," *Sierra Club Bulletin,* January 1896, 282–83.)

240

The eager throng is pushing blindly northward in mad excitement. Every one is anxious to get ahead, jumping and grinding against one another like bowlders in flood time swirling in a pothole. ("John Muir on the Sea," *San Francisco Examiner,* August 23, 1897. The Klondike gold rush.)

241

It is a fine thing to see people in dead earnest about anything. Even so dull a business as gold-getting may be interesting. Nature scatters grains of gold in gravel beds, and so the laziest crowds rotting in cities spring to life and are scattered over the farthest wildernesses to make way for civilization. The right

ministry of wealth is blessed, and one must admire the energy
of those who seek it in the face of cold, hunger and self-denying
toil. But in the search many become insane and strike about
blindly in fierce excitement, moved more by the mere lust of
wealth than appreciation of its right use. ("John Muir on the
Sea," *San Francisco Examiner*, August 23, 1897. The Klondike
gold rush.)

242

A little money we all need nowadays, but there is nothing
about the getting of it that should rob us of our wits. Gold
digging is only a dull chore, and no sane man will allow it
to blind him and draw him away from the real blessings
of existence. Life is too short to allow much time for money-
making. ("John Muir on the Sea," *San Francisco
Examiner*, August 23, 1897. The Klondike gold rush.)

243

. . . While the fortunes of the few who strike it rich are
repeated and re-echoed over and over again, the thousands
who fail and vanish in the wilderness like raindrops in the sea
are seldom noticed. ("John Muir on the Sea," *San Francisco
Examiner*, August 23, 1897. The Klondike gold rush.)

244

The forests of America, however slighted by man, must have
been a great delight to God; for they were the best He ever
planted. ("The American Forests," *Atlantic Monthly*, August
1897, 145; *ONP*, 331.)

245

. . . Sequoias, kings of their race, growing close together
like grass in a meadow, poised their brave domes and spires
in the sky three hundred feet above the ferns and the lilies that
enameled the ground; towering serene through the long
centuries, preaching God's forestry fresh from heaven.
("The American Forests," *Atlantic Monthly*, August 1897, 146;
ONP, 334.)

246

Every other civilized nation in the world has been compelled to care for its forests, and so must we if waste and destruction are not to go on to the bitter end, leaving America as barren as Palestine or Spain. ("The American Forests," *Atlantic Monthly,* August 1897, 147; *ONP,* 337.)

247

. . . Our government . . . is like a rich and foolish spendthrift who has inherited a magnificent estate in perfect order, and then has left his fields and meadows, forests and parks, to be sold and plundered and wasted. . . . ("The American Forests," *Atlantic Monthly,* August 1897, 148; *ONP,* 340.)

248

. . . Timber-thieves of the Western class are seldom convicted, for the good reason that most of the jurors who try such cases are themselves as guilty as those on trial. ("The American Forests," *Atlantic Monthly,* August 1897, 149; *ONP,* 343–44.)

249

Uncle Sam is not often called a fool in business matters, yet he has sold millions of acres of timber land at two dollars and a half an acre on which a single tree was worth more than a hundred dollars. ("The American Forests," *Atlantic Monthly,* August 1897, 151; *ONP,* 348.)

250

The outcries we hear against forest reservations come mostly from thieves who are wealthy and steal timber by wholesale. ("The American Forests," *Atlantic Monthly,* August 1897, 155; *ONP,* 360–61.)

251

Even in Congress, a sizable chunk of gold, carefully concealed, will outtalk and outfight all the nation on a subject like forestry. . . . ("The American Forests," *Atlantic Monthly,* August 1897, 156; *ONP,* 361.)

252

Emerson says that things refuse to be mismanaged long.
An exception would seem to be found in the case of our forests,
which have been mismanaged rather long, and now come
desperately near being like smashed eggs and spilt milk.
("The American Forests," *Atlantic Monthly*, August 1897, 156;
ONP, 361–62.)

253

Any fool can destroy trees. They cannot run away; and if they
could, they would still be destroyed,—chased and hunted down
as long as fun or a dollar could be got out of their bark hides,
branching horns, or magnificent bole backbones. ("The American
Forests," *Atlantic Monthly*, August 1897, 157; *ONP*, 364.)

254

God has cared for these trees, saved them from drought,
disease, avalanches, and a thousand straining, leveling tempests
and floods; but he cannot save them from fools,—only Uncle
Sam can do that. ("The American Forests," *Atlantic Monthly*,
August 1897, 157; *ONP*, 365.)

Nature Ever at Work

1897–1899

255

. . . When I heard the storm I made haste to join it; for in storms nature has always something extra fine to show us. . . . ("An Adventure With a Dog and a Glacier," *Century Magazine*, September 1897, 771; *SKN*, 22.)

256

At such times one's whole body is eye, and common skill and fortitude are replaced by power beyond our call or knowledge. ("An Adventure With a Dog and a Glacier," *Century Magazine*, September 1897, 774; *SKN*, 54. Crossing an ice bridge over a crevasse.)

257

The man who said, "The harder the toil the sweeter the rest," never was profoundly tired. ("An Adventure With a Dog and a Glacier," *Century Magazine*, September 1897, 776; *SKN*, 70.)

258

Even medicine chests may be found in Yukon packs. The idea of carrying medicine to Alaska where all the wilderness is medicine! As well take drugs to heaven. ("Trails of the Gold Hunters," *San Francisco Examiner*, October 1, 1897.)

259

All the world is sprinkled with gold, but precious sparsely in most places. Nature, it seems, put just enough of the exciting stuff into the starry mass to keep people on the move. ("Pathless

Treasure Fields of the Frozen Northland," *San Francisco Examiner*, October 11, 1897.)

260

God never made an ugly landscape. All that the sun shines on is beautiful, so long as it is wild. . . . ("The Scenery of California," *California Early History: Commercial Position: Climate: Scenery.* San Francisco: California State Board of Trade, 1897, 16. This strong statement in a little-known state promotional brochure appeared later in a watered-down and grammatically incorrect version in a prominent periodical and a major book. "None of Nature's landscapes are ugly so long as they are wild. . . . " *Atlantic Monthly*, January 1898, 17; *ONP*, 4.)

261

Thousands of tired, nerve-shaken, over-civilized people are beginning to find out that going to the mountains is going home; that wildness is a necessity; and that mountain parks and reservations are useful not only as fountains of timber and irrigating rivers, but as fountains of life. ("The Wild Parks and Forest Reservations of the West," *Atlantic Monthly*, January 1898, 15; *ONP*, 1.)

262

Awakening from the stupefying effects of the vice of over-industry and the deadly apathy of luxury, they are trying as best they can to mix and enrich their own little ongoings with those of Nature, and to get rid of rust and disease. Briskly venturing and roaming, some are washing off sins and cobweb cares of the devil's spinning in all-day storms on mountains. . . . ("The Wild Parks and Forest Reservations of the West," *Atlantic Monthly*, January 1898, 15–16; *ONP*, 1–2.)

263

Few in these hot, dim, frictiony times are quite sane or free; choked with care like clocks full of dust, laboriously doing so much good and making so much money,—or so little,—they are no longer good for themselves. ("The Wild Parks and Forest Reservations of the West," *Atlantic Monthly*, January 1898, 16; *ONP*, 3.)

264

How many hearts with warm red blood in them are beating under cover of the woods, and how many teeth and eyes are shining! A multitude of animal people, intimately related to us, but of whose lives we know almost nothing, are as busy about their own affairs as we are about ours. . . . ("The Wild Parks and Forest Reservations of the West," *Atlantic Monthly*, January 1898, 21; *ONP*, 16.)

265

. . . It is far safer to wander in God's woods than to travel on black highways or to stay at home. ("The Wild Parks and Forest Reservations of the West," *Atlantic Monthly*, January 1898, 25; *ONP*, 28.)

266

Bears are a peaceable people, and mind their own business, instead of going about like the devil seeking whom they may devour. ("The Wild Parks and Forest Reservations of the West," *Atlantic Monthly*, January 1898, 25; *ONP*, 28.)

267

No American wilderness that I know of is so dangerous as a city home "with all the modern improvements." ("The Wild Parks and Forest Reservations of the West," *Atlantic Monthly*, January 1898, 25; *ONP*, 28.)

268

One should go to the woods for safety, if for nothing else. ("The Wild Parks and Forest Reservations of the West," *Atlantic Monthly*, January 1898, 25; *ONP*, 28.)

269

If every citizen could take one walk through this [Sierra] reserve, there would be no more trouble about its care; for only in darkness does vandalism flourish. ("The Wild Parks and Forest Reservations of the West," *Atlantic Monthly*, January 1898, 27; *ONP*, 33–34.)

270

Camp out among the grass and gentians of glacier meadows, in craggy garden nooks full of Nature's darlings. Climb the mountains and get their good tidings. Nature's peace will flow into you as sunshine flows into trees. The winds will blow their own freshness into you, and the storms their energy, while cares will drop off like autumn leaves. ("Yellowstone National Park," *Atlantic Monthly,* April 1898, 515–16; *ONP,* 56.)

271

As age comes on, one source of enjoyment after another is closed, but Nature's sources never fail. Like a generous host, she offers here brimming cups in endless variety, served in a grand hall, the sky its ceiling, the mountains its walls, decorated with glorious paintings and enlivened with bands of music ever playing. ("Yellowstone National Park," *Atlantic Monthly,* April 1898, 516; *ONP,* 56.)

272

Fears vanish as soon as one is fairly free in the wilderness. ("Yellowstone National Park," *Atlantic Monthly,* April 1898, 516; *ONP,* 57.)

273

You may be a little cold some nights, on mountain tops above the timber-line, but you will see the stars, and by and by you can sleep enough in your town bed, or at least in your grave. ("Yellowstone National Park," *Atlantic Monthly,* April 1898, 517; *ONP,* 59.)

274

. . . See how God writes history. No technical knowledge is required; only a calm day and a calm mind. ("Yellowstone National Park," *Atlantic Monthly,* April 1898, 517; *ONP,* 59.)

275

If tree-lovers could only grow bark and bread on their bodies, how fine it would be, making even handbags useless! (Letter to Charles Sprague Sargent, June 7, 1898; *LAL,* vol. 2, 310.)

276

The inhabitants are going to towns to work in factories and stores, seeking fortunes—they know not how. They look down on labor. Health, manhood are all given away for the sake of something beyond their reach, and which even if attained would be found far less desirable by any sane person than the home farm life they despise. (Massachusetts, October 1898; *JOM,* 368.)

277

In my first interview with a Sierra bear we were frightened and embarrassed, both of us, but the bear's behavior was better than mine. ("Among the Animals of the Yosemite," *Atlantic Monthly,* November 1898, 617; *ONP,* 174.)

278

One touch of nature makes the whole world kin. . . . ("Among the Birds of the Yosemite," *Atlantic Monthly,* December 1898, 753; *ONP,* 218.)

279

. . . Many of the wanderers are shot for sport and the morsel of meat on their breasts. Man then seems a beast of prey. Not even genuine piety can make the robin-killer quite respectable. Saturday is the great slaughter day in the bay region. . . . Over the fine landscapes the killing goes forward with shameful enthusiasm. After escaping countless dangers, thousands fall, big bagfuls are gathered, many are left wounded to die slowly, no Red Cross Society to help them. Next day, Sunday, the blood and leggins vanish from the most devout of the bird butchers, who go to church, carrying gold-headed canes instead of guns. After hymns, prayers, and sermon they go home to feast, to put God's song birds to use, put them in their dinners instead of in their hearts, eat them, and suck the pitiful little drumsticks. It is only race living on race, to be sure, but Christians singing Divine Love need not be driven to such straits while wheat and apples grow and the shops are full of dead cattle. Song-birds for food! Compared with this, making kindlings of pianos and violins would be pious economy. ("Among the Birds of the Yosemite," *Atlantic Monthly,* December 1898, 759–60; *ONP,* 237–38.)

The last sentence of that quotation was used at least twice earlier, being reworked each time. ". . . Better make stove-wood of pianos to feed the kitchen fire." ("The Yosemite Valley," *Picturesque California*, 1888, 194.) "Better far, and more reasonable, it would be to burn our pianos and violins for firewood, than to cook our divine midgets of song larks for food." ("Save the Meadow Lark," *San Francisco Daily Morning Call*, March 24, 1895.)

280

The game scout reported a few bear and reindeer tracks, but saw none of the animals. He was left to look out for game but to shoot none, only to be ready to point it out to the game fellows, that they might have the pleasure of making a hole in the animals, shedding the blood, satisfying the savage instincts that should be kept down rather, after civilization has gone far enough for trousers and prayers. (Cruising with the Harriman Alaska Expedition, July 19, 1899; *JOM*, 413.)

281

Nature is ever at work building and pulling down, creating and destroying, keeping everything whirling and flowing, allowing no rest but in rhythmical motion, chasing everything in endless song out of one beautiful form into another. ("Yosemite National Park," *Atlantic Monthly*, August 1899, 152; *ONP*, 97.)

282

Remember your penitential promises. Kill as few of your fellow beings as possible and pursue some branch of natural history at least far enough to see Nature's harmony. (Letter, August 30, 1899, to Mary and Cornelia Harriman and Elizabeth and Dorothea Draper, girls who were on the Harriman Alaska Expedition. *LAL*, vol. 2, 333.)

Everyone Needs Beauty

1900–1912

283

The warm, brooding days are full of life and thoughts of life to come, ripening seeds with next summer in them or a hundred summers. ("The Wild Gardens of the Yosemite Park," *Atlantic Monthly*, August 1900, 177; *ONP*, 165.)

284

Nature's tables are spread and fires burning. You must go warm yourselves and eat. (Letter to Mrs. Richard Swain, October 21, 1900; *LAL*, vol. 2, 337.)

285

It is always interesting to see people in dead earnest, from whatever cause, and earthquakes make everybody earnest. ("Fountains and Streams of Yosemite National Park," *Atlantic Monthly*, April 1901, 564; *ONP*, 264.)

286

No true invitation is ever declined. ("Hunting Big Redwoods," *Atlantic Monthly*, September 1901, 316; *ONP*, 320.)

287

Happy nowadays is the tourist, with earth's wonders, new and old, spread invitingly open before him, and a host of able workers as his slaves making everything easy, padding plush about him, grading roads for him, boring tunnels, moving hills out of the way, eager, like the Devil, to show him all the kingdoms of the world and their glory and foolishness, spiritualizing travel for him with lightning and steam, abolishing space and time and almost everything else. Little children and tender, pulpy people, as well as storm-seasoned explorers, may now go almost everywhere in smooth comfort, cross oceans and deserts scarce accessible to fishes and birds, and, dragged by steel horses, go up high mountains, riding gloriously beneath starry showers of sparks, ascending like Elijah in a whirlwind and chariot of fire. ("The Grand Cañon of the Colorado," *Century Magazine*, November 1902, 107; *STT*, 347.)

288

Nearly all railroads are bordered by belts of desolation. ("The Grand Cañon of the Colorado," *Century Magazine*, November 1902, 107; *STT*, 348.)

289

Every feature of Nature's big face is beautiful,—height, hollow, wrinkle, furrow, and line. . . . ("The Grand Cañon of the Colorado," *Century Magazine*, November 1902, 108; *STT*, 352.)

290

. . . like trees in autumn shedding their leaves, going to dust like beautiful days to night, proclaiming as with the tongues of angels the natural beauty of death. ("The Grand Cañon of the Colorado," *Century Magazine*, November 1902, 116; *STT*, 380.)

291

. . . As we go on and on, studying this old, old life in the light of the life beating warmly about us, we enrich and lengthen our own. ("The Grand Cañon of the Colorado," *Century Magazine*, November 1902, 116; *STT*, 382.)

292

. . . Everybody needs beauty as well as bread, places to play in and pray in, where Nature may heal and cheer and give strength to body and soul. This natural beauty-hunger is displayed in poor folks' window-gardens made up of a few geranium slips in broken cups, as well as in the costly lily gardens of the rich, the thousands of spacious city parks and botanical gardens, and in our magnificent National parks. . . . Nevertheless, like everything else worth while, however sacred and precious and well-guarded, they have always been subject to attack, mostly by despoiling gain-seekers,—mischief-makers of every degree from Satan to supervisors, lumbermen, cattlemen, farmers, eagerly trying to make everything dollarable, often thinly disguised in smiling philanthropy, calling pocket-filling plunder "Utilization of beneficent natural resources, that man and beast may be fed and the dear Nation grow great." Thus long ago a lot of enterprising merchants made part of the Jerusalem temple into a place of business instead of a place of prayer, changing money, buying and selling cattle and sheep and doves. ("The Hetch- Hetchy Valley," *Sierra Club Bulletin*, January 1908, 217; *YOS*, 256–57. A less adequate version of this appeared two months earlier: "The Tuolumne Yosemite in Danger," *The Outlook*, November 2, 1907, 488.)

293

In these ravaging money-mad days monopolizing San Francisco capitalists are now doing their best to destroy Yosemite Park, the most wonderful of all our great mountain national parks. ("The Hetch-Hetchy Valley," *Sierra Club Bulletin*, January 1908, 211.)

294

That anyone would try to destroy such a place seems incredible; but sad experience shows that there are people good enough and bad enough for anything. ("The Hetch-Hetchy Valley," *Sierra Club Bulletin*, January 1908, 219; *YOS*, 260–61.)

295

Landscape gardens, places of recreation and worship, are never made beautiful by destroying and burying them. ("The Hetch-Hetchy Valley," *Sierra Club Bulletin*, January 1908, 219; *YOS*, 260.)

296

These temple destroyers, devotees of ravaging commercialism, seem to have a perfect contempt for Nature, and, instead of lifting their eyes to the God of the mountains, lift them to the almighty dollar.

Dam Hetch-Hetchy! As well dam for water-tanks the people's cathedrals and churches, for no holier temple has ever been

consecrated by the heart of man. ("The Hetch-Hetchy Valley,"
Sierra Club Bulletin, January 1908, 220; *YOS,* 261–62.)

297
Bathed in such beauty, watching the expressions ever varying
on the faces of the mountains, watching the stars, which here
have a glory that the lowlander never dreams of, watching the
circling seasons, listening to the songs of the waters and winds
and birds, would be endless pleasure. And what glorious
cloud-lands I would see, storms and calms, a new heaven and
a new earth every day. ("Cathedral Peak and the Tuolumne
Meadows," *Sierra Club Bulletin,* January 1911, 2.)

298
In the whole Sierra there isn't a sneeze, but I was quite unable
to convince Emerson that this was so. . . . You can't take cold if
you keep your nose out of doors. (From a talk given by Muir in
New York, June 17, 1911; *Sierra Club Bulletin,* January 1924,
45–46.)

299
. . . All Nature's wildness tells the same story: the shocks
and outbursts of earthquakes, volcanoes, geysers, roaring,
thundering waves and floods, the silent uprush of sap in plants,
storms of every sort, each and all, are the orderly, beauty-
making love-beats of Nature's heart. ("Three Adventures in the
Yosemite," *Century Magazine,* March 1912, 661; *YOS,* 86.)

300
All the world was before me and every day was a holiday, so
it did not seem important to which of the world's wildernesses
I first should wander. (1912; *YOS,* 3–4.)

301
Yosemite was all one glorious flower garden before plows
and scythes and trampling, biting horses came to make its wide
open spaces look like farmers' pasture fields. (1912; *YOS,* 148.)

Looking Back

1912

302

Boys are often at once cruel and merciful, thoughtlessly hard-hearted and tender-hearted, sympathetic, pitiful, and kind in ever-changing contrasts. Love of neighbors, human or animal, grows up amid savage traits, coarse and fine. ("My Boyhood," *Atlantic Monthly,* November 1912, 580; *BAY,* 23–24.)

303

Old-fashioned Scotch teachers spent no time in seeking short roads to knowledge, or in trying any of the new-fangled psychological methods so much in vogue nowadays. There was nothing said about making the seats easy or the lessons easy. We were simply driven point-blank against our books like soldiers against the enemy, and sternly ordered, `Up and at 'em. Commit your lessons to memory!" If we failed in any part, however slight, we were whipped; for the grand, simple, all-sufficing Scotch discovery had been made that there was a close connection between the skin and the memory, and that irritating the skin excited the memory to any required degree. ("My Boyhood," *Atlantic Monthly,* November 1912, 582–83; *BAY,* 32–33.)

304

. . . A black eye could never be explained away from downright fighting.

A good double thrashing was the inevitable penalty, but all without avail: fighting went on without the slightest abatement, like natural storms, for no punishment less than death could quench the ancient inherited belligerence in our pagan blood.

("My Boyhood," *Atlantic Monthly*, November 1912, 583; *BAY*, 33–34.)

305

. . . By the time I was eleven years of age, I had about three fourths of the Old Testament and all of the New by heart and by sore flesh. I could recite the New Testament from the beginning of Matthew to the end of Revelation without a single stop. (1912; *BAY*, 31; *LAL*, vol. 1, 26–27.)

306

This sudden plash into pure wilderness—baptism in Nature's warm heart,—how utterly happy it made us! Nature streaming into us, wooingly teaching, preaching her glorious living lessons, so unlike the dismal grammar ashes and cinders so long thrashed into us. Here, without knowing it, we still were at school; every lesson a love lesson, not whipped, but charmed into us. ("Plunge into the Wilderness," *Atlantic Monthly*, December 1912, 814; *BAY*, 62–63.)

307

Everything new and pure in the very prime of the spring when Nature's pulses were beating highest, and mysteriously keeping time with our own! ("Plunge into the Wilderness," *Atlantic Monthly*, December 1912, 814; *BAY*, 63–64.)

308

Think of the millions of squabs that preaching, praying men and women kill and eat, with all sorts of other animals great and small, young and old, while eloquently discoursing on the coming of the blessed, peaceful, bloodless millennium! Think of the passenger pigeons that fifty or sixty years ago filled the woods and sky over half the continent, now exterminated by beating down the young from their nests together with the brooding parents, before they could try their wonderful wings; by trapping them in nets, feeding them to hogs. . . . None of our fellow mortals is safe who eats what we eat; who in any way interferes with our pleasures; or who may be used for work or food, clothing or ornament, or mere cruel, sportish amusement. Fortunately many are too small to be seen, and therefore enjoy life beyond our reach. And in looking through God's great stone

books made of records reaching back millions and millions
of years, it is a great comfort to learn that vast multitudes of
creatures, great and small and infinite in number, lived and
had a good time in God's love before man was created.
("Plunge into the Wilderness," *Atlantic Monthly,* December 1912,
818; *BAY,* 83–84.)

309

When tired we dare not even go to the spring for water in the
terrible thirst of the muggy dog-days, because the field was in
the sight of the house and we might be seen. . . . We had to make
ourselves sick that we might lay up something against a sick
day, as if we could kill time without injuring eternity. (1912;
LAL, vol. 1, 46. "As if you could kill time without injuring
eternity." *Walden,* Henry David Thoreau.)

310

A stitch in time saves nine, so we take a thousand stitches
to-day to save nine to-morrow. (1912; *LAL,* vol. 1, 46.)

311

We might live free, rich, comfortable lives just as well as not.
Yet how hard most people work for mere dust and ashes and
care, taking no thought of growing in knowledge and grace,
never having time to get in sight of their vast ignorance. (1912;
LAL, vol. 1, 50.)

312

Good walkers can go anywhere in these hospitable mountains
without artificial ways. But most visitors have to be rolled on
wheels with blankets and kitchen arrangements. (Letter to
Howard Palmer, December 12, 1912; *LAL,* vol. 2, 379.)

313

In those early days . . . it often seemed to me that our fierce,
over-industrious way of getting the grain from the ground was
closely connected with grave-digging. The staff of life, naturally
beautiful, oftentimes suggested the grave-digger's spade. Men
and boys, and in those days even women and girls, were cut
down while cutting the wheat. The fat folk grew lean and the
lean leaner, while the rosy cheeks brought from Scotland and

other cool countries across the sea, soon faded to yellow, like the wheat. We were all made slaves through the vice of over-industry. ("Lessons of the Wilderness," *Atlantic Monthly,* January 1913, 89; *BAY,* 222–23.)

314

. . . Even when sick, we were held to our tasks as long as we could stand. . . . Only once was I allowed to leave the harvest-field—when I was stricken down with pneumonia. . . . No physician was called, for father was an enthusiast and always said and believed that God and hard work were by far the best doctors. ("Lessons of the Wilderness," *Atlantic Monthly,* January 1913, 89; *BAY,* 224; *LAL,* vol. 1, 48.)

315

Wildness was ever sounding in our ears, and Nature saw to it that besides school lessons some of her own lessons should be learned, perhaps with a view to the time when we should be called to wander in wildness to our heart's content. (March 1913; *BAY,* 49–50.)

316

. . . No fire can be hotter than the heavenly fire of faith and hope that burns in every healthy boy's heart. (March 1913; *BAY,* 77.)

317

Of the many advantages of farm life for boys one of the greatest is the gaining a real knowledge of animals as fellow-mortals, learning to respect them and love them, and even to win some of their love. Thus godlike sympathy grows and thrives and spreads far beyond the teachings of churches and schools, where too often the mean, blinding, loveless doctrine is taught that animals have neither mind nor soul, have no rights that we are bound to respect, and were made only for man, to be petted, spoiled, slaughtered, or enslaved. (March 1913; *BAY,* 109–10.)

318

Like Scotch children in general we were taught grim self-denial, in season and out of season, to mortify the flesh, keep our bodies in subjection to Bible laws, and mercilessly punish ourselves for every fault imagined or committed. (March 1913; *BAY*, 130.)

319

Most wild animals get into the world and out of it without being noticed. Nevertheless we at last sadly learn that they are all subject to the vicissitudes of fortune like ourselves. (March 1913; *BAY*, 134.)

320

[Redwing blackbirds each] enjoys an exhilarating feast, and after all are full they rise simultaneously with a quick birr of wings like an old-fashioned congregation fluttering to their feet when the minister after giving out the hymn says, "Let the congregation arise and sing." (March 1913; *BAY*, 142.)

321

The muskrat is one of the most notable and widely distributed of American animals, and millions of the gentle, industrious, beaver-like creatures are shot and trapped and speared every season for their skins, worth a dime or so—like shooting boys and girls for their garments. (March 1913; *BAY*, 180–81.)

322

Surely a better time must be drawing nigh when godlike human beings will become truly humane, and learn to put their animal fellow mortals in their hearts instead of on their backs or in their dinners. (March 1913; *BAY*, 181.)

323

All hale, red-blooded boys are savage, the best and boldest the savagest, fond of hunting and fishing. But when thoughtless childhood is past, the best rise the highest above all this bloody flesh and sport business, the wild foundational animal dying out day by day, as divine uplifting, transfiguring charity grows in. (March 1913; *BAY*, 181.)

324

. . . Surely all God's people, however serious and savage,
great or small, like to play. Whales and elephants, dancing,
humming gnats, and invisibly small mischievous microbes—all
are warm with divine radium and must have lots of fun in them.
(March 1913; *BAY,* 186–87.)

325

Making some bird or beast go lame the rest of its life is a sore
thing on one's conscience, at least nothing to boast of, and it has
no religion in it. (1913; *JOM,* 438.)

Death is a Kind Nurse

1913–

326

This grand show is eternal. It is always sunrise somewhere; the dew is never all dried at once; a shower is forever falling; vapor is ever rising. Eternal sunrise, eternal sunset, eternal dawn and gloaming, on sea and continents and islands, each in its turn, as the round earth rolls. (1913; *JOM*, 438.)

327

I only went out for a walk, and finally concluded to stay out till sundown, for going out, I found, was really going in. (1913; *JOM*, 439.)

328

The winds wander, the snow and rain and dew fall, the earth whirls—all but to prosper a poor lush violet. (1913; *JOM*, 439.)

329

Death is a kind nurse saying, 'Come, children, to bed and get up on the morning'—a gracious Mother calling her children home. (1913; *JOM*, 440.)

330

The wrongs done to trees, wrongs of every sort, are done in the darkness of ignorance and unbelief, for when light comes the heart of the people is always right. ("Save the Redwoods," *Sierra Club Bulletin*, January 1920, 2.)

331

No doubt these trees would make good lumber after passing through a sawmill, as George Washington after passing through the hands of a French cook would have made good food. ("Save the Redwoods," *Sierra Club Bulletin,* January 1920, 2.)

332

. . . In every walk with Nature one receives far more than he seeks. (*STT,* 128.)

Index